New
ADHD
Medication Rules

Brain Science & Common Sense

Dr. Charles Parker

SPECT Brain Imaging Consultant,
Author of Deep Recovery,
Functional Systems Medicine Consultant,
Author of CorePsych Blog
Neuroscience Consultant,
Child Adolescent and Adult Psychiatrist

NEW YORK
VIRGINIA

NEW NEW ADHD MEDICATION RULES

BY DR. CHARLES PARKER

Copyright © 2010 by Dr. Charles Parker, Second Edition

ISBN 9781938467226

CoreBrain Books

Published by

an imprint of Morgan James Publishing

212-574-7939
www.koehlerbooks.com

Publisher
John Köehler

Executive Editor
Joe Coccaro

In an effort to support local communities, raise awareness and funds, Morgan James Publishing donates a percentage of all book sales for the life of each book to Habitat for Humanity Peninsula and Greater Williamsburg.

Get involved today, visit www.MorganJamesBuilds.com

*The real voyage of discovery consists
not in seeking new landscapes,
but in having new eyes.*

Marcel Proust

ACKNOWLEDGEMENTS

This book could not find its way to your hands without significant support and help from a number of people, present both in my current life and from years past. To name but a few: Thomas Walker, English instructor at Culver Military Academy; Herman Belmont MD, director of child psychiatry at Hahnemann Medical College who encouraged my first medical writing experience; the many interesting reps and regional directors at Shire Pharmaceuticals who supported the many speaking and learning opportunities with medical colleagues for many years as a national speaker for Shire.

(Pharmaceutical companies have contributed considerably to the public good, and it is most disconcerting to see how they have suffered by default at the hands of so many who simply don't appreciate the importance of understanding the basic science or ongoing medical communication in that dinner meeting context.)

I also offer a special note of appreciation for the trust and patience of the many interesting patients over the years who helped me understand what the books don't teach. If you know the science, the meds work more predictably.

Specific deep gratitude goes out to an outstanding fellow writer and stand-up commentator on the challenges we all face with the evolution of ADHD treatment, Gina Pera in San Francisco, author of the award winning *Is it You, Me or Adult A.D.D.?*. Others who helped me to complete *Rules* include Marianne Sunderland, Betsy Davenport, and Tom Walker, that same remarkable teacher from high school fifty years ago who returned to help with a final review.

Most especially, thanks to my wife, Cate, for her patience with personal time for this project, as I'm admittedly often writing and editing CorePsych Blog and *Rules* at the expense of our time together. Without Cate working to keep the home fires burning, *Rules* would still be just an idea.

Table of Contents

Introduction

Pills have to pass through your body before they reach your brain. The body is uniformly overlooked. What happens along that complex journey determines a drug's effectiveness and predictability.

Unfortunately, far too many significant problems exist with Attention Deficit Hyperactivity Disorder meds because those who prescribe them don't consider or grasp the ways drugs are absorbed and then processed in the bowel, liver or the brain itself. A patient's diet, medical status and allergies are given only modest consideration. The interactions of multiple medications also are given short shrift. Instead, physicians often base dosages on broad —- even vague -- medication formulas. Too many prescribe from statistical averages, not individual needs.

Succinctly: too many simply are not paying attention to the meds for paying attention.

What I hope to accomplish through this book is to enlighten my medical colleagues and embolden patients suffering with ADHD or symptoms masquerading as an attention or hyperactivity disorder.

My intention is to arm patients, or those caring for them, with enough critical information to at least ask their doctors informed questions and challenge limited conventional thinking.

Much of the information presented here is highly scientific. Some of it is anecdotal, and the rest is clearly advocacy. It's my firm belief, after spending decades treating those struggling with emotional and mental illnesses, that treatments should be customized based upon available science. Most importantly, physicians and patients need to partner in treatments so that medications can be adjusted correctly.

The wrong mix of drugs or prescriptions in the wrong amounts can be deadly. They can tip someone with depression into suicide. They can exacerbate, rather than alleviate, hyperactivity. The wrong blends or amounts of drugs can harm rather than heal.

ADHD diagnosis and treatment strategies are tricky to begin with. Technology has advanced to a point where it's now possible to read the brain's reaction to drugs and to find in the body root causes for previously unpredictable problems. Yet, too few physicians are willing or capable of employing these new assessment techniques. Treatments are not on a par with current, easily available brain science, leaving a global quandary about viable ADHD practice strategies.

ADHD medications don't work like slap shots in a penny arcade. They must be exact with laser accuracy to hit their intended targets. Too many with ADHD are treated with cookie-cutter medication recipes and diagnoses based upon superficial behavioral appearances that overlook the complexity of the human brain. What's missing is applied neuroscience discoveries; years of brain scan data and biomedical evidence should drive more effective diagnosis and medication delivery.

My hope is that *New New ADHD Medication Rules* raises awareness of better and more sophisticated approaches to treating and diagnosing ADHD.

Why Rules And Why Me?

I've witnessed medical denial all over the country. After speaking nationally to thousands of doctors, nurses and mental health professionals since first starting to practice in the 1970s, I've come to important conclusions: Too many don't want to listen to the neuroscience data; too many are focused on those superficial, often counterproductive DSM 4/5 labels; too many docs hurry to prescribe ADHD meds without considering real consequences.

Regrettably, some of the most pressing medical denial and defensive, self-righteous thinking exists in otherwise sophisticated metropolitan communities with the most prestigious medical academic institutions. Ironically, some of the most intelligent and otherwise well-informed communities, such as Boston, New York City and San Francisco, shun new medical information unless it comes from their in-town provincial, group-think establishment thought leaders.

I've watched their responses to my presentations over the years, and repeatedly experienced their determined resistance to thoughtful investigation and improved intervention strategies. Intellectual egoism rules, serves to neglect critical thinking, and shrouds progress in wrappings of doctrinaire beliefs that don't match biomedical brain evidence. The outcome of these blinders is that you, the patient, from New York to South Africa, suffer the consequences of ineffective or potentially dangerous treatments.

Experience Matters

In a word, *Rules* arises from more than forty years of practice feedback from patients, especially when I didn't get the meds right following the most approved protocols. I listened, and I looked for additional answers and more evidence-based approaches. *Rules* summarizes that learning history.

I've repeatedly interviewed thousands of clients who suffered for years at the hands of denial and medical innocence. After a hasty diagnostic process, too few medical providers show interest in expectations of how the meds work in the first place, or how they should work most effectively in the long run. For example, many think understanding interactions between stimulants and other medications is a waste of time and inconsequential, despite the fact that it can result in suicidal thinking.

Repeated clinical experiences provoked me to reveal to the public, specifically ADHD sufferers, the dangers and shortcomings of the status quo and its dated practices.

My hope is that *Rules* stimulates patients and conscientious medical practitioners to improve the consideration of treatment alternatives. ADHD dogma will be exposed and public sentiment will hopefully encourage individual challenges to the current medical establishment. By reading *Rules,* I hope you will become one of the informed who will ultimately pressure treatment providers to break from mainstream thinking and adapt more comprehensive ADHD diagnosis and treatment options. Let's work together to encourage a revolution in awareness that will mandate reforms to the way medical professionals evaluate and treat this disorder.

Don't be intimidated by the science here or the medical jargon. I will attempt to make it as clear as possible. However, some of what you will read is very technical. It's important to understand the biological and chemical bedrock upon which *Rules* is based. My goal is to present comprehensive alternatives for easily workable, everyday medication management. Details matter and the ADHD details in *Rules* rely on applied street smarts and common sense.

On the Brighter Side

Improved ADHD medications work remarkably well and with reassuring predictability. These drugs have been studied, researched and written about more than any other children's medications. Meds are safe when used correctly and often work well with both children and adults. Simply follow the *Rules* and medication outcomes will significantly improve.

ADHD treatments provide one of the best ways to understand the mix of co-existing problems so often seen with ADHD. Symptomatic treatment chasing superficial appearances often misses underlying reasons for diagnostic and treatment failures.

Side effects with ADHD meds can point the way for even better care if you understand all of the underlying conditions, not just the surface symptoms. These next examples will give you a glimpse of some of the topics covered later in more detail.

1. A ten-year-old boy with inattention and clear symptoms on a commonly used ADHD rating scale starts an immediate release medication: Adderall IR [Immediate Release]. He is given the medication in the morning, but doesn't get a noon dose because he does not want others to know about his problems by going to the school nurse. His morning is great, but his afternoon

is terrible with interruptions and misbehavior. The summary from the teachers: "The medication is not working." The action from the doctor: Increase the morning dose to cover the afternoon time by raising the Adderall IR. Outcome: Now he is furious and wild in the morning and crashes even more furiously in the afternoon. Often the next reflex recommendation: "The medication is not working correctly – get rid of it." **My conclusion:** No, it *is working exactly as expected*; it was, however, *adjusted incorrectly*. He is significantly overdosed, toxic in the morning, and still is not adequately dosed in the afternoon. *Adderall IR doesn't last more than five-to-six hours with correct dosing -- dosage for more than that duration is simply too much.*

2. An adult male is promoted at work, is pleased with his new responsibilities, but continues to feel increasingly overwhelmed by the complexity of "administrative problems" with colleagues. He was an outstanding performer when he had control over his work duties, but feels increasingly overwhelmed. He loses sleep, feels more inundated, fears losing his job in an uncertain economy, is given antidepressants and deteriorates dramatically. He was treated for ADHD as a child, but following this episode of reacting to the antidepressant he is quickly labeled "bipolar," and is now regularly thinking of suicide. *Antidepressants can make ADHD worse, and can make ADHD look like a mood disorder.* **My conclusion:** He does suffer from ADHD, which

is aggravated by the change of context[1] at work, and can be quickly corrected with proper medication management. Adult psychiatrists are often suspicious and misinformed about adult ADHD treatment because many lack the basic training for ADHD diagnosis and medication management.

3. A wealthy technology consultant is suicidal, feels that he is demented, and, at age forty five, fears he may suffer from an early onset of Alzheimer's. He has been treated by several psychiatrists over the years, suffers with ADHD and depression, and comes to the office for a second opinion after having been diagnosed with "brain injury" by the initial SPECT imaging consultants. He is on Prozac and Adderall, and his SPECT brain images look like brain Swiss cheese. **My conclusion:** Brain injury is not the problem – he is demented from a common drug-drug interaction with Adderall and Prozac. Prozac interacts by building up the Adderall, through blocking the Adderall breakdown. He is simply toxic, and needs different doses of new medications. His ADHD, anger and depression are treatable through correcting the inappropriate mix of medications. His SPECT consultants missed the drug interaction and mistook the diminished functioning as brain injury.

4. An apparently healthy adolescent girl, attractive and outgoing, cannot seem to find the correct dosage

---

1 - Context: The circumstances that form the setting for an event or idea in terms that can be assessed more objectively.

of stimulant medication. As she has grown older her periods are worse than ever, prompting a start on birth control. The stimulants are either too weak to correct her attention issues, or too strong and make her overwhelmingly anxious. She skips breakfast, sleeps only about six hours on average, and, quite surprisingly, has bowel movements only two times a week.

My conclusion: After careful review she shows many characteristics of a narrow Therapeutic Window[2] encouraged by multiple metabolic issues associated with Polycystic Ovarian Syndrome, gluten sensitivity, and delayed bowel transit time, *all of which significantly interfere with stimulant medications.* Sleep, nutrition, neurotransmitter challenges, hormone dysregulation[3] and significant metabolic[4] slowing all contribute to unpredictable outcomes with ADHD medications. ADHD medications simply can't be adjusted correctly without understanding and correcting each underlying biologic-based metabolic, burn rate variable.

The bottom line: medication management using stimulants can be achieved by paying more attention to the associated medication effects so often found with ADHD problems. If you don't look, you simply can't see. If you do look, recognizing these remarkably simple patterns will make ADHD medication management much more predictable.

We must start paying closer attention to both the person

2 - See Chapter 6 for specifics on this important Window phenomenon.
3 Imbalance
4 Rate the medication is used by the body

and his reaction to stimulant medications. And this bears repeating: remember, misusing stimulants can result in severe consequences, including suicide.

Too many with ADHD suffer the consequences of physician errors in dosing strategies, missed diagnosis and confusion over treatment objectives. Much of the bad rap, the pervasive stigma, associated with the diagnosis and treatment of ADHD is based upon failures to identify these many problems.

It's quite paradoxical that ADHD, one of the most common psychiatric conditions, is pervasively misidentified and mismanaged. Many patients justifiably complain. Regrettably, they too often conclude that the treatment process is useless, or they remain frustrated for years with problematic or inadequate treatment.

Far too often, ADHD patients find themselves not only misunderstood by their family, but also lost in a sea of medication confusion within the medical community. Lacking obvious and specific rules to address the complexity of their symptoms, many feel they must rely on vague intuition or the advice of gossip. In fact, the meds often appear so unpredictable that many, at first, seriously doubt the stimulant medication choice, the medication dosage, and the underlying ADHD diagnosis from the outset. Too often it seems like nothing works, no matter what interventions physicians offer.

In the courtroom, hearsay evidence is inadmissible. When it comes to medical strategies, however, "hearsay" forms the bulk of how a condition is judged and treated. They act upon something mentioned casually by a friend, or something heard in a brief news report. In our new Twitter world, hearsay is becoming a mainstay. When it comes to ADHD treatment, everyone is an expert, and unreliable gossip sets the standard of care. Unfortunately, some health care professionals also plug into this pattern of gossip. Speculation rules far too often, even in the treatment community.

The truth is, current practices typically make little operational sense to patients or many professionals. Translating ADHD medication theory into effective what-you-do-in-the-office, step-by-step guidelines remains downright elusive. Even the most informed observer recognizes that no rule book exists that sets clear treatment options, clear objectives, and specific outcome measures.

Treating ADHD without first establishing targeted outcome expectations is like playing basketball without hoops; there's a lot of running around with no goal. Often treatment appears as a "maybe," an afterthought, with casual consideration.

New, more brain-physiology-precise ADHD guideposts remove much of the guesswork. I have found such testing more precise than psychological testing, which can muddle ADHD diagnosis, burdening a medical team with uncertainty because their own psychological criteria remain uncertain.

Why is there so much denial regarding precise use of stimulant medications, and how have we become collectively so inattentive to the details for correctly dosing stimulant medications? It's all about training, perspective, and the evolution of measurement tools based upon brain and body biologic processes.

Our Shared Past Medical Perspective

In 1969, when I started training in Philadelphia, the two essential questions all psychiatric residents were instructed to ask every new patient were, "What are your dreams?" and, "What are your fantasies?" Our highly regarded psychoanalytic instructors in those days were simply not interested in biology and often opposed medical interventions. They were even against talking too much with the patients because you might interfere with the transference.[5] This remarkable bias *against biological understanding* remains alive and well in consultation practices across the US even today.

Why? Psychiatrist's back then did not have access to adequate measurements. The tools to evaluate brain function simply did not exist for street practitioners. Without laboratory measurements for brain activity, specifically the way the brain and body actually work together, the standard of care was not based upon biological evidence and relied, instead, on psychological explanations.

In those days, it was like dealing with microbes without benefit of a microscope. You don't think about looking for what you can't see.

Brain and Body Science Changed the Treatment Game

ADHD treatment is at a crucial crossroads. We can now see more brain activity markers than ever before. Science is taking us down dramatically different diagnostic paths. Those following the scientific trail find themselves in a growing controversy about standards of ADHD medical care. The public, medical research teams and the media now hotly debate the subject of correct ADHD treatment.

---

5 - Transference: Projecting the unconscious past onto the therapist - requiring a "blank slate" from the therapist to facilitate that process.

Brain science has yielded so much new information that many providers are scrambling to try to keep up with data regarding functional brain activity, nutrition, and the great variety of treatment options available for the ADHD spectrum of difficulties.

On the other hand, when treating ADHD in the office, many others attempt to navigate the direct effects of challenged brain function without specific maps or a compass. Most psychological tests and questionnaires don't provide specific medication treatment markers that can be used in everyday office management. And, more importantly, psychological testing itself often overlooks specific functional brain challenges that result in ADHD symptoms.

We need more dynamic, more applicable, measurable markers for every office visit, for every medication check, that serve both patients and practitioners.

Patients need an uncomplicated method by which they can easily report progress. Patient involvement in care must become much more participatory, more highly refined at every medication check. A recent study[6] regarding topics discussed during medication checks showed that only one minute of an average sixteen minute office visit was spent discussing medication effectiveness. An essential, yet frequently overlooked example question: "Exactly how long does that stimulant medication actually work?" One unstructured office visit every one-to-three months will not provide the answer.

Research clearly shows that we aren't on target in the office. Static diagnostic labels based upon appearances don't adequately address moving mind dynamics. We plainly aren't

6 Findling RL, et al, J *Atten Disorder* 2009:1-9

thinking about the way the brain is working, the way it actually functions cognitively, as observed in the office. We aren't thinking about thinking.

Brain and Body Science Evolve

Those old psychological questions about dreams and fantasies remain useful in specific circumstances, but the prevailing medical focus is now on developing measurable biologic evidence, beyond dreams and imagination. New biological inquiries about metabolic dysfunction[7] become imperative, because body metabolism, including hormonal function, immune dysfunction and the body's rate of metabolism, all directly affect brain function: measurable unbalanced behaviors in thinking, feeling and acting. You probably already knew that; but what you likely didn't know is that measurement tools such as laboratory and imagining methods have significantly improved.

You can see the manifestations of unbalanced brain function in the office and in the street any day, but only laboratory tools will reveal specifics about the biological occurrences that send those unbalanced signals and result in changes with brain activity -- now measurable on a cellular level.

If we can now identify and then measure thinking, feeling and acting behaviors that associate with specific brain functions, and then relate them to specific brainwork, why are we still using superficial terms and measures that document appearances in the office as the ADHD standard of care? Terms such as "hyperactive and inattentive" are observations and descriptions of behavior, not statements about real brain function. These

7 Dysfunction: cellular and brain physiology simply don't work the way they should

outdated terms work as markers only for the least informed, and then inadequately if the patient begins treatment with stimulant medication. Those diagnostic targets are simply too vague.

New Brain Maps Do Change the Treatment Process

Patients must become familiar with these completely different levels of thinking with their respective medical consultants. *Rules* shows you how to effectively participate in your own treatment.

Our work together must better identify specific treatment targets, provide improved clinical diagnostic measurements, create measurements easy to use during brief medication checks, and identify specific medication actions and interactions. The devil is in those details, and we're too often collectively lost without them.

Think of the ADHD treatment game we have been using in the past as Golf ADHD, and this new game, with different rules, as Tennis ADHD. Golf ADHD is not a bad game; it simply is insufficient in many cases to deal with the new biologically based feedback loops we will be outlining in these next chapters. Golf ADHD Rules may work for the most uncomplicated presentations, while Tennis ADHD Rules apply with any additional complexity, with nuanced problems that don't respond to ordinary care. These new perspectives aren't to discard past ADHD labels, only to suggest future treatment protocols based upon greater precision available with the new brain and body science.

Let's get started with a different game.

Chapter I
Right Drugs for the Right Diagnosis

The experimenter who does not know what he is looking for
will not understand what he finds.

Claude Bernard, Physiologist

B rain function in any individual with ADHD is infinitely more
complex than the three current subtypes of "hyperactive,
inattentive and combined." While useful in a limited context,
these three labels are actually shallow subsets, representing
what I call "appearance labels" -- how a behavior looks on the
outside.

Adult ADHD was slow to be recognized because the medical community long ago defined the condition as only associated with "physical hyperactivity." The trouble now is that only a small percentage of adults and children manifest physical hyperactivity. Actually, when I started my training in child psychiatry the diagnosis was "Minimal Brain Dysfunction" and the patient had to have actual neurologic signs, like an atypical spastic gait, to meet the criteria for ADHD.

The thinking then was that since the observed fidgetiness tended to fade by adulthood, the condition itself would disappear. Instead, we now know that individuals become more mentally hyperactive, and less physically hyperactive, as they grow into adulthood. Moreover, we've learned that even children can display not a bit of hyperactivity and still have significant ADHD. As science has deepened our awareness of ADHD we're rapidly abandoning one-dimensional, less dynamic, superficial descriptors.

Regrettably, many health professionals still follow these outdated, simplistic descriptive labels, words that don't touch the humanity or the person, much less the complex behaviors associated with patterns of the brain activity revealed even upon a casual interview.

The current ADHD Diagnostic Statistical Manual, called DSM-4R, creates an often cloudy set of surface criteria, creating significant confusion about medication management. Fortunately, we now have access to more specific hard-data objectives that correlate with new findings in brain and body science. These findings coordinate well with the remarkable advances in psychopharmacology,[8] and make the entire

---

8 The use of medications and supplements for psychiatric difficulties

medication management process more predictable.

ADHD Diagnosis Involves
More Than a Description of Behavior

ADHD is a specific, biologically-based brain dysfunction, not a personality trait, and certainly not a character disorder or a symptom of willfulness. It's a result of mixed internal brain and body activities. ADHD processing problems dwell much deeper than the three official subtypes' names might indicate: "hyperactive," "inattentive" and "combined." ADHD is far more complex than "fidgeting" or "daydreaming" or some descriptive combination thereof.

Many still ask anyway: "Am I ADD or AD*H*D?" Just remember, those old labels are lifeless, and won't help you target your real disorder. You are far more than a label, and even "ADHD" doesn't nearly cover the complexity, the variables that should be on the treatment/observation table. And the most important point: that label often won't get you where you want to go. Static labels do create imprecise targets.

These outdated terms focus far more on observable behaviors, and with the new brain science we are far beyond surface appearances. In these next chapters I'll show you how we can augment those limited behavioral assessments with office questions that reveal brain function -- actual brain/cognitive/thinking activity -- instead of those limited findings with observable, superficial motor activity.

Medical Imprecision In the
Current Treatment Process

First, it's helpful to start with the easy and sometimes useful tip of the ADHD iceberg: what it looks like on the surface. Description *is* useful, but should be the *beginning* of the inquiry, not the end. After that surface grid is set, we can take a deep dive beneath the water and further delineate the complexity of dangerous underwater structures that so frequently impede essential navigation. Remember, it wasn't the tip of the iceberg that sank the Titanic.

Diagnosis By Medication: To Be Avoided

Moreover, ADHD diagnostic processes should involve much more than an experiment with medications. Too many say that ADHD diagnosis is easily accomplished with a "trial of stimulant medication." In other words, if you get better, you have ADHD. Recent studies have confirmed that such an inappropriate approach is completely unfounded scientifically. Such a capricious "diagnostic" process is completely unacceptable, no matter who suggests it, and is an example of the widespread diagnostic confusion -- looking for appearance answers.

ADHD diagnoses present a challenge much more involved than, "It's either this or that." The question isn't whether you are inattentive or hyperactive -- what you look like. The more precise array of questions must drive deeper and identify the underlying brain function condition.

The obvious question that follows: without clear diagnostic targets, without a bullseye to aim for, how can we determine if we have hit the mark? Exactly what is the target for addressing challenges with "inattention" and how do we better discuss it with our physician? More accurately, what are all of the targets?

Most psychiatric problems are the result of more than one simple diagnosis. Because of this complexity, a broad net of multiple medical considerations should be cast. Among many other issues, ADHD medications don't correct:

Hormone imbalance

Malnutrition

Depression

Lead toxicity

Immune dysfunctions

Depleted neurotransmitters

Stimulant medications used to treat ADHD can exacerbate the symptoms of brain injury, and can seriously aggravate depression to the point of suicidal thinking. ADHD has been viewed as a "simple" condition instead of a highly complex one, with much variability person to person.

Sometimes ADHD medications work for a short period, even for the "wrong" disorder. For example, adrenal fatigue will respond to stimulant medication for "cognitive exhaustion" in the short run, but requires much higher doses of stimulants in the long run, with potential catastrophic results. Wrong medication for the wrong diagnosis creates deterioration in the presenting condition.

Over time, however, even medications that show promise often don't work consistently, or may actually worsen cognitive/ thinking problems. At this point, the physician and patient often enter a long-term pattern of feeling as though nothing is working right. In fact, nothing is working because, again, they're aiming at the wrong target.

Beyond Descriptive Diagnosis for ADHD

What exactly are we treating when we treat ADHD? If we

don't know precisely what we are looking for, we will not find it, or might mistake it for something else.

If we build a house without a foundation, just throwing up studs and drywall, it won't endure over time. Functional diagnosis, an understanding of the brain and body's physical systems which form the basis for ADHD symptoms and behaviors, should build the foundation of treatment. Nailing on medications should occur down the line, after the functional brain diagnostic foundation is poured and solid.

The Diagnostic Importance of Context: Reality Does Change

One of the most indispensable observations regarding our life experience is that the real world regularly changes over time. We lose a parent. A child becomes critically ill. Stress mounts at work. The economy takes a dive. It rains before our picnic. Reality changes. ADHD treatment that worked before might not withstand the added stress of changing reality.

Most of our relationship difficulties arise from an elemental misunderstanding of our relationship with nature, time and change. As we become accustomed to cars, air conditioning and warm homes, we often assume that we can control nature and natural events, even death.[9] In the short term, we may appear to have beaten the natural system. Science and labels have taken us to this measure of relative safety, denial, and limited appreciation for the passage of time and changes in reality.[10]

Many professionals still believe that ADHD diagnosis presents as symptomatic, actually active, around the clock. But,

---

9 Becker, E *The Denial of Death* 1997
10 Parker, C, *Deep Recovery* 1992

in fact, ADHD symptoms appear in certain reality circumstances, but not in others. What flairs up at work may not show itself at home. Each place and time is characterized by different contexts, different levels of predictability and structure. Even predictable structures manifest change, but they often change more slowly and predictably over time.

ADHD is a Contextual Disorder

Here's the scientific explanation:

The prefrontal cortex uses "working memory" to organize reactions to change. An oversimplification will help: "working memory" is a three-part process that separates us from dogs, cows and even well-trained elephants. First, we see the problem, cognitively think about it, and tag that reality. Second, we move to fix it or do something with the reality. Third, we carry that memory, that training process of reality management, into the next day. 2+2=4 is an example of working memory that we use in daily activities. We see the 2, add [action] the second 2, and carry the result into tomorrow. With ADHD problems and the subsequent working memory compromise, ADHD can even impair 2+2. Yes, elephants and dogs can be trained for these activities, but only in specific limited circumstances.

And for working memory to work effectively, it must be *synchronized*. Without synchronization the brain feels like short circuits or molasses. Synchronization is like dancing to the beat. Without synchronization those with ADHD don't step to the beat of reality. They hear the drum but step on their partner's feet, and hate themselves for it. Those who suffer with ADHD just can't dance in certain circumstances, certain realities, but often can dance quite well in others.ADHD diminishes that working memory by slowing the prefrontal cortex, and with the brain in life, even milliseconds count. Here's a list of some circumstances that can trip this dynamic imbalance in any life experience:

Increased Variables: More things to do than expected

Decreased Structure: No specific support or clear rules

No Stimulating Focus: Work is neither exciting or interesting

It's not uncommon to see ADHD flair up as college freshmen struggle in their new reality. They're overwhelmed with work, no longer have the structure imposed from living at home, and can lose interest in studies through distraction -- increased variables, decreased structure, no stimulating focus.

The "It Depends on Context" Diagnosis

If you suffer with ADHD, the more balls life throws at you, the more you'll experience a decrease in function, unless you love the excitement (stimulating focus) like driving an ambulance. It'll get worse, too, if your cognitive supports (sleep, exercise, diet, a relationship with a friendly, operational prefrontal cortex) start slipping as well. The symptoms also shift with age as cognitive abilities may ebb as well.

ADHD Diagnostic Context Reminders

ADHD intensifies with stress, such as rapidly increasing variables.

ADHD occurs in specific context/environments, such as home or work.

ADHD occurs in the context of specific biomedical realities, such as gluten sensitivity.

ADHD patterns most frequently show up in the context of real change, during transitions in life, such as divorce, changing schools.

ADHD symptom intensity changes over time and real circumstances, such as job mastery over time.

ADHD is most frequently expressed in specific symptoms that involve thinking patterns in a specific context, such as an increase in parties, too often called social anxiety.

ADHD is much more than a problem with academic performance and school. Home has much less structure and more unpredictable realities, with the consequence of increased symptoms of ADHD in that reality, that context.

Biomedical, Hard Data Assessments For Diagnosis

Hard data for molecular and cellular dysfunctions that aggravate ADHD symptoms, and slow the prefrontal cortex, is increasingly available, from neurotransmitter evaluations to functional brain imaging such as SPECT.

SPECT brain imaging opens wide the ADHD diagnostic door to considering other revealing laboratory assessments such as hormone or immune dysfunctions. If you understand the clinical significance of SPECT imaging, and are seeking more precise answers, you will inevitably find yourself drilling down even deeper for more specific answers.

I have seen remarkable improvements by measuring biomarkers for neurotransmitters, immune dysfunction and hormone challenges. Subsequent interventions will often reduce dependence on psychiatric medications.

Summary On Diagnostic Evidence

New brain and body laboratory and brain-scan discoveries tell us more about ADHD and the multiple possible associated conditions.

Functional neuroimaging and new information regarding the biologic processes of brain function is changing the medication process.

Diagnosing ADHD solely from superficial description and appearances often doesn't provide an adequate biologic target for resolution of symptoms.

SPECT and fMRI imaging is useful in the diagnosis and treatment of ADHD symptoms.

ADHD is a contextual problem, occurring in the context of changing circumstances.

The brain is connected to the body, the endocrine system, the immune system, the many other neurotransmitters, and the overall state of nutrition-- all of which are now measurable. Biomedical imbalances add to any ADHD problems.

Measure these other biological contributory factors to help with refractory[11] diagnoses, even those treated for years.

---

11 Refractory: Not responsive to treatment

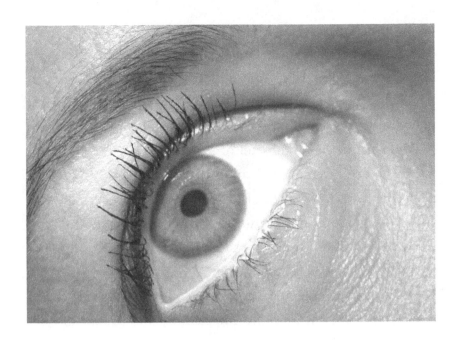

Chapter 2
How To Get Past Outward Appearances

Efficiency is doing things right;
effectiveness is doing the right things.

Peter Drucker, Management Consultant

Sailing off the rocky coast of Maine, you encounter constantly changing conditions. The sea and land press together. The tide, the moon, the wind, the barometric pressure, the temperature, and the billow of the sail combine to modify the location of the sailboat. Many variables are at play and constantly change.

Within just a few moments, you can be on the rocks, or in smooth waters. The same applies to ADHD meds. Each medication measurement, each medication check, should work in concert to keep you off the rocks. Why sail without a telltale (wind indicator), a Fathometer or a map?

If you are given a medication that is supposed to last for a specific period of time, but lasts only a few hours, how will you know what to expect during the course of a day? More importantly: were you told exactly what to expect with the duration of that specific medication at the outset?

Fortunately, once properly selected and dosed, ADHD medications often work quite consistently and predictably, so the challenge with medication management is often more like sailing on a calm bay than a storm-tossed sea. But no matter what the weather, the best navigation is indispensable.

Office Diagnosis for ADHD: Thinking and Acting

Clinically, ADHD is a problem of thinking and acting out of sync with reality. Working memory, discussed above, can become desynchronized. There might be problems with not thinking before acting, or there might be problems with thinking without acting. "Out of sync" is just that: out of sync. Reality is in your face, and you're either coping with it incorrectly, or not in a timely fashion. You're out of beat with reality.

Those who suffer with ADHD live in after beats, stepping on the toes of dancing partners, family members and close colleagues, indeed the world. They remain *out of sync* with the "ready, aim, fire" brain activities of thinking and acting in the context of changing reality.

These new "functional" (cognitive/thinking) criteria I'm about to describe relate to "thinking and acting" in a way that can easily be measured in the office. Desynchronized behaviors reveal the underlying ADHD issues. Each ADHD subset described below notes what looks on the outside like an "attention deficit" of a specific, office-measurable brain-activity level. Interestingly, with more in a moment, so many of these ADHD challenges reside downstream from an "attention abundance" that looks to the untrained eye like an "attention deficit" from the outside.

While anyone may occasionally lose timing, ADHD sufferers are too often stuck in counterproductive repetition of these patterns that reveal in specific realities. They are stuck in time. One part works, the other doesn't, or neither works correctly. The three common functional ADHD-related brain activities are these (with more details in the following chapters):

Acting ADHD: Acting Without Thinking, the old standard with impulsivity as the "functional" common denominator. This is impulsivity spelled out in specific action and, of course, in specific reality context. "Hyperactivity" is at once too global and too restrictive, and diminishes the complexity of the ADHD by looking only at behavior, not the underlying brain function.

Thinking ADHD: Thinking without acting, the most frequently missed subset, confused with OCD. Way too much thinking and not enough appropriate action. Synonyms: Unmanageable cognitive abundance, attention abundance disorder. This presentation does not exist in the current DSM 4, and most certainly will not be found in DSM 5.

Avoiding ADHD: Not acting and not thinking, the least common and the next most frequently missed, especially in adolescence and adults. They wish to avoid change. They can't deal with reality, often because they hate the possibility of obvious brain desynchronization -- it's embarrassing. This finding can be found in the DSM 4 only as a personality disorder, avoidant personality. Almost always Avoiding ADHD can be corrected with accurate diagnosis and treatment.

These three subsets provide a more precise measure of exactly what you're shooting at with medications. The current problem with diagnosis -- hyperactivity, inattention and combined -- is simply too vague to work with in the office, unless clinicians are only going for the more limited, less precise, behavioral change.

Summary: The Functional Diagnostic Process

Report these contextual observations to your medical team. Recognize changes in your life that could affect you.

Go beyond questionnaires to build feedback loops and identify clear targets necessary for medication adjustments.

Using these transparent, easy identification tools places you, the patient, more fully on the medical team.

Use these parameters/understandings with children as discussion points. This practice will in the office provide them with a sense of self-esteem and self-mastery, instead of uninformed submission to vertical, adult medical authority. Your doctors will appreciate your understanding and input.

Compliance and evolved discussion regarding treatment objectives with your medical partnership travels longer over time than superficial directions with no appreciation of the brain process you're trying to correct.

Chapter 3
Acting ADHD:
Acting Without Thinking

If you can't describe what you are doing as a process,
you don't know what you're doing.

W. Edwards Deming, Management Consultant

During my adult psychiatric training in Philadelphia, one resident constantly interrupted to make inappropriate, sometimes humorous, comments.   The meeting topic, no matter what the focus of the teaching moment, no matter the seriousness of the content, was repeatedly set aside for his inane remarks. They were impulsive, not hyperactive. His interruptions impeded his own development.

Acting Without Thinking: Some people might call this ADHD, a predominately hyperactive subtype. ADHD individuals may appear as physically hyperactive, but beyond obvious physical actions (foot jiggling while seated, getting up frequently while seated, jangling car keys, etc.), they may simply blurt impulsively, even buy something impulsively.

Acting ADHD presents as an "impulsive pattern" that is not necessarily purely physical hyperactivity. Because we now think only in description, and "inattention" is not easily measured or observed in the office, many, even now, believe that "hyperactivity" is the only ADHD subset. Other, subtler, impulsivity characteristics, so commonplace, have been overlooked.

Missing the varieties of impulsivity can create lifelong problems. I have seen hundreds of adults whose ADHD symptoms were missed in childhood because impulsivity was not on the radar at that time, and, in some physicians' and therapists' offices, it's still not on the radar. Missing this diagnosis leaves adults crippled and indeed developmentally arrested as they have trouble moving to increasingly demanding adult responsibilities.

In those with Acting ADHD, actions precede thinking. Often the actions, existing outside the dampening effect of thinking, are out of step with the context of social or interpersonal reality. Individuals with this set of challenges may be:

1. Acting – can't sit still
2. Feeling – angry outbursts

3. Thinking – repeating ideas

Some comedians may appear to display these impulses, but their action are controlled and premeditated. The context wherein comedians may truly meet ADHD criteria is offstage, where there is less scripting and markedly decreased structure. On stage, variables are predictable, structure is clear and they have repeatedly practiced their structured shticks.

In children, "hyperactivity" appears as a nearly continuous stream of action. But with a few years of age, and growing brain development of the pre-frontal cortex, many find interests, focus and apparent relaxation when performing certain tasks. Working memory may also improve. The subsequent conclusion: They must not be suffering with ADHD because symptoms "come and go" under differing circumstances. So often we hear, "He couldn't have ADHD. He plays video games all day." And, "He grew out of it." The inaccurate assumption: because it doesn't present all of the time, it's gone; because it occurs only in certain contexts, it's gone.

When we're establishing treatment targets, we can include "repeatedly acting inappropriately" as a clear "impulsive" ADHD target. Once we do that, the impulsivity pattern becomes much easier to identify, in whatever context.

If impulsivity in later years appears time and again in the context of specific changing realities, and is found to be associated with a previous history of ADHD in childhood, it makes more sense to consider ADHD as a likely diagnosis. It's treatable, but only if you find it!

Interestingly, Acting ADHD is currently the most easily understood marker. Even though some mistakenly think that all ADHD involves hyperactivity, it accounts for only 20% of ADHD problems. The other 80% are described next, here, and are the most frequently missed subsets.

Take a moment here to just think of the challenging consequences of acting without thinking, and trace back the context, the life-reality where it popped up, then consider that context: increased variables, decreased structure, without a focus.

The pattern will become clearer with your own examples.

Chapter 4
Thinking ADHD: Thinking Without Acting

If you do not know how to ask the right question,
you discover nothing.

W. Edwards Deming, Management Consultant

Thinking without acting, Thinking ADHD, is far more prevalent than any of the ADHD subsets, and repeatedly overlooked, with substantial emotional and economic consequences. Ever know anyone who simply could not decide on anything? Remember when you were a kid and one of your classmates repeatedly asked you what you were going to do so they could decide what they would do? Have you ever considered those plagued by indecision may be "cognitively dependent" -- instead of co-dependent or emotionally dependent?

Thinking, thinking, thinking, and then thinking some more, and acting just too late, or not at all, can smother a lifetime. Think: college applications. To the untrained eye, this type of ADHD looks like "OCD,"[12] and is often misdiagnosed as such. Without a doubt, Thinking ADHD is the most frequently overlooked subset. Almost everybody -- even many clinicians -- thinks this presentation is Obsessive Compulsive Disorder, and it does at first appear so from the description. But remember, we're leaving superficial descriptors behind and looking at the underlying way the brain works, the way their mind works, and their subsequent behavior. And OCD demonstrates that a focus, a topic, a behavior, is not so pervasive and widespread throughout one's life experience.

Overthinking is associated with what looks like "brain hyperactivity" in the office. Thinking rather than acting is the result of uncontrolled mental over-activity and, most often, associated with specific brain inactivity in the inferior orbital prefrontal cortex on SPECT scans during concentration.

My initial recognition of Thinking ADHD, back in 1996, ultimately led me to work with Daniel Amen, author of *Healing ADD*[13] in 2003. In his book, Amen had the SPECT brain image evidence to back up that subset of Thinking ADHD findings.

Here is what overthinking can look like:

Jane has convinced herself that her overthinking works.

---

12 Obsessive Compulsive Disorder
13 Amen, D, *Healing ADD, The Six Subtypes of ADD* 2002

She thinks she's being "deliberate" and "careful" in her decision making. Husband, Jack, can attest that she will "think" of a solution for months that could be solved in twenty minutes. Many who suffer with relentless thinking are convinced that overthinking is constructive and even commendable. But their spouses will attest that overthinking is a significant problem that can stress a marriage. It becomes an unending cycle that parasitically feeds on itself and the unhappy victim.

Thinking ADHD can appear as four different subsets:

- **Physically restricted:** Becoming homebound because physically leaving involves too many decisions in that different reality.

- **Emotional overthinking:** Worrying, fretting, and obsessing about insignificant details.

- **Cognitively[14] overthinking:** Mind-stuck, unable to decide, often not "worried" but constantly always "preoccupied" and "spaced," indecisive, overwhelmed, "mental."

- **Compulsively decisive:** In a profound paradoxical effort to preclude thinking, we see this pattern in strong vertical managers functioning inadequately at home, yet over-controlling in meetings at the office. "We're done with thinking and need to take action." Often they evolve into ineffective micromanagers who shun feedback and seek pervasive control.

Unmanageable Cognitive Abundance: Over the Top Thinking

Most Thinking ADHD is often mistaken for bipolar, anxiety, social anxiety, even dementia, and is often linked to real

---

14 Purely mental, having to do with only thinking, not feeling.

memory and sleep problems. The mind can't focus because the brain is disorganized, and the brain itself appears cognitively hyperactive. This subsequent type of "brain constipation" often looks like dementia, and may be associated with metabolic issues that significantly affect brain function. Many practitioners misdiagnose this brain overactivity as "neurotoxicity." But the apparent "toxicity" can originate from simply too many thoughts and may or may not be associated with brain injury, or a toxic condition. Another way to think about this Thinking ADHD phenomenon: brain spaghetti -- too much, all entwined.

Dangerous: Thinking ADHD -
Missed Diagnosis And Suicide

I have observed Thinking ADHD since 1996, and can attest to thousands of individuals interviewed with these problems of missed/incorrect ADHD diagnosis. In my practice I see about 1000 new patients each year, and then all of our team sees them for years after. Many have suffered with this Thinking ADHD as a missed diagnosis for years, for decades, some for a lifetime.

If "worry" is identified as a chief complaint by the patient, that worry is often first treated as depression. SSRIs, the first choice of meds for obsessional anxiety, have been recommended by the American Psychiatric Association as a primary treatment for "anxiety" for years -- and still are.

However, if the true origin of "worrying" is simply a blatant, cognitive symptom of Thinking ADHD, the use of SSRI medications, without recognizing this associated condition of Thinking ADHD, will significantly complicate treatment and can result in dangerous depression -- even suicidal thinking. SSRIs help with affective, feeling anxiety, but almost always make thinking/cognitive anxiety worse -- they aggravate ADHD.

The SSRI medications recommended as "standard care" for Obsessive Compulsive Disorder (OCD) and other repetitive thinking conditions simply do not work effectively for ADHD subsets. In fact, SSRIs often exacerbate Thinking ADHD problems, leading to mood swings and even suicide attempts. At the very least the patient feels untreatable with antidepressants.

The most frequent outcome of this tragically missed, simple diagnosis is the addition of another new, often incorrect, diagnosis of bipolar disorder. The moods become unmanageable, the impulsivity increases because the SSRIs decrease the effective damping of the prefrontal cortex, and the patient is incorrectly treated with mood stabilizers -- not once in a while -- often.

Warning: SSRIs Can Dangerously Worsen Thinking ADHD

If you get worse with antidepressant medications, it does not absolutely mean you have bipolar disorder, or other mood disorder diagnoses. As you likely know, mood stabilizers simply do not correct ADHD. Again, the frequency of ongoing incorrect office trials with incorrect medications for years often heralds a consequence of staggering self-defeat. Low self-esteem intensifies as the Thinking ADD persists, because it is not identified or treated correctly. Here is what it looks like:

Cognitive anxiety
Obsessional thinking (sometimes solved by compulsive doing)
Substance abuse

Unmanageable cognitive abundance

Thinking worries

Sleep disorder

Brain constipation

Overthinking

Indecision

Overwhelmed with pressures

Cognitive depression with apathy and indifference

Developmental arrest

Confusion

Memory impairment

Job insecurity

Low self-esteem

Feeling like an impostor

Asperger's Syndrome

Ideas of reference (the TV is talking directly to you)

Autism/Asperger's

Paranoia

Borderline personality

Avoidant personality

Social anxiety

Passive-aggressive personality

Workaholism

Wrecked by success

Mutism

Apraxia

Word finding

Bipolar Disorder

Overthinking Turns Deadly:
Suicide Becomes The Only "Out"

Suicidal action may become the ADHD person's only perceived choice to turn their brain off. They feel completely misunderstood, minds still racing, and see no way out. However, deeper thinking, deeper analysis of the possible ADHD challenges often will save the day.

Death is not an acceptable solution to a simple short-term ADHD problem that can significantly improve, often in only a day or two with proper medical intervention. This possible link to suicide is so important, and so frequently missed, that it's my main reason for writing this book. I have personally seen this danger thousands of times, not just a few hundred. If you look for it, you will see it.

Repeat: SSRIs Can *Increase* Suicide Risk with ADHD

SSRIs do not successfully treat ADHD thinking; in fact, they aggravate it. They may help with the associated affect, the moods and the frustration, but they don't correct cognitive abundance. They do fix the depression, but at the same time will often aggravate the mental confusion. Poor mental performance and the feeling of inability to think can be profoundly discouraging as one seeks to advance his or her station in life, especially after paying all that money for medical visits and new antidepressants.

SSRIs can make you feel crazy and make ADHD worse. *I repeat.* SSRIs can make pre-existing suicidal ideas much worse if the ADHD is not simultaneously treated.

Indecisive ADHD: Stuck On Thinking

They overthink and worry, but can't decide, just can't make

up their minds. They often marry "a prefrontal cortex -- a brain with administrative functions." They need an executive function, a decision maker, because they can't decide, can't turn off their brain, can't sleep with their thoughts, and rarely can discuss conflicts -- simply because they have never decided how they actually feel about matters. If you're emotionally close to them, they will tell you they often don't know who they are.

They can't tell you they love you simply because they are thinking too much, and must have a categorical, one hundred percent answer to be honest. They frequently have a feeling of acting as an impostor; no one knows their "true identity" or understands the unbelievable mental pressures that live behind a mask of confidence.

The mental indecision process can become so overwhelming that they can't think for themselves, have no political opinion, don't read the paper, and tend to listen to and participate in gossip rather than form their own view on a variety of matters. Their thought patterns look like a serious case of frozen thinking, with vacuous staring. They are often compulsively self-reflective, with no direction. They have little or no sense of self, and can't answer their spouses when they ask, "Do you really care about me?" Caring is too big a question. Just what is "caring" anyway? Could you be more specific?

Their marriages often don't last, and they can't move ahead in their work because a change in structure will become overwhelming, and they will be wrecked by their own success.

This type of Thinking ADHD looks very OCD, and in everyday practice is often associated with symptoms "described" as OCD, but, as noted, these people will respond poorly over time to an SSRI. SSRIs are the current first line of treatment for OCD.

The Resentful Follower

These folks are also quite resistant to therapy because they don't want, in fact can't stand, more thinking. Yet, they do well with ADHD coaching and cognitive interventions that help with prefrontal-executive organization of thinking. Their behavior makes them seem like resentful followers. They can exist for a lifetime as a resentful follower that relentlessly hates following.

They can't make decisions, and often ask for help, then resent help when it comes or often refuse it. Here's their familiar lament: "I can't decide, I won't do it now, and, by the way, don't you tell me what to do either. Leave me alone, but don't go away."

"Grumpy" Lives!

I have a patient who for years thought of himself jokingly as Grumpy, one of the Seven Dwarfs with Snow White. He wore Grumpy T-shirts, in fact had a dozen of them, and Grumpy caps and was always lost at home with his wife, in spite of the fact that he did well in the structure and predictable variables of work. Often he isolated himself in his garage workshop, and remained Grumpy almost all the time.

He did well in the structure of the military (remember structure and that military-reality context can diminish reactive thinking) and succeeded as a Navy master chief. He was depressed, always felt like a loser, and stayed away from crowds; they were unpredictable, and he hated small talk. Trials of SSRIs left him feeling stoned and "out of it." He had refused psychotherapy many times.

Treating the Thinking ADHD and the depression simultaneously, the SSRI meds worked on his depression, while the ADHD was being treated effectively with other stimulant medication. The master chief found himself more typically the Happy Dwarf with his new perspective. Now he can socialize, and is no longer dependent at home on his wife giving directions. The cognitive, Thinking ADHD and the depression needed separate treatment to be successful with each subset of diagnostic challenges. He no longer feels alone with himself.

The stimulant medications dramatically fixed the Thinking ADHD, and he confirmed he "never felt this good in my entire life." Now he can really laugh at that old Grumpy guy.

Decisive ADHD:
Impulsive Decisions As A Coping Strategy

Some with Thinking ADHD manage to avoid overthinking and relentless worry by forcing premature, pressured decisions. They avoid the thinking confusion by completely bypassing it. They are micromanagers. They want to end the meeting after they've had their say, simply because they are avoiding any possibility of overthinking.

Their functional objective is to turn off their minds. These individuals will often say that they have no trouble with thinking. They don't worry because they refuse to think, and then often worry they will get caught up in the thinking process. They appear to be decision makers. Often they are unbalanced vertical managers. They simply can't let any more variables in and are threatened by others who ask questions.

I've worked with a few physicians who are "vertical micro-managers." They have a "you kiss the ring," "I'm the boss!" mentality.

They hire family for executive positions and encourage the team to think of themselves as family, but they frequently can't successfully navigate interpersonal relationships. Again, they don't want treatment; too many more messy variables to overwhelm them. Nothing is ever right. They are often angry because the existence of others around them creates additional thinking. Personal interactions require thought. They want to be done with thinking, almost at any cost, even losing a job or a marriage. Simple example: "I refuse to think too much, and will make this decision now and stick by it; no discussions, no matter what -- and remember -- all the decisions are mine."

Both Indecisive and Decisive forms of Thinking ADHD are often associated with drug and alcohol abuse, and addictions of any kind, including work. The rush of mind-altering drugs temporarily turns off the mind, as do other types of serious injury such as fighting or sexual addiction. Pain or pleasure rushes subdue thinking. I have met some powerful people with these obvious symptoms. They are often workaholics, and often unhappy with the structural limitations of marriage and personal commitment.

At work they are often in control. At home they often are not and resent the inevitable interpersonal deficits associated with the unpredictable variables of real intimacy.

"Wrecked by Success" or
Overwhelmed with New Duties?

Interestingly, Sigmund Freud wrote a "character"[15] paper published in 1916 titled Those Wrecked by Success.[16] There

---

15 Character: A diagnosis for those who appear free from obvious emotions: anxiety or depression

16 Freud, S. (1916). Some Character-Types Met with in Psycho-Analytic Work. *The Standard Edition of the Complete Psychological Works of Sigmund Freud*, Volume XIV (1914-1916): 309-333.

he described, quite carefully, this same overthinking subset of ADHD in post-Victorian Vienna. Even in those early days of psychiatry, he recognized that some successful people are actually wrecked, undone by their own success, in spite of looking symptom-free before their newly added responsibilities. But Freud missed the biologic part of the picture; he didn't have our new brain technology.

Individuals who become successful with a prior mild foundation of "too much thinking," often become considerably worse when they attain new responsibilities. A car salesman, for example, is great at selling cars on the lot, but has difficulty coping -- and succeeding -- as a manager working inside an office and dealing with various interpersonal relationships. There are too many people with too many variables, too many decisions and no rehearsed structure.

That salesperson-turned-manager appears to be wrecked by success. But he is actually wrecked by more variables, including the fact that the structure is one he hasn't himself created. He has to go back to selling cars; he just can't survive in the complexity of the office, even though he is one of the sharpest salesmen at the dealership. "Smart" doesn't necessarily mean "functional in every life circumstance." He was "decisive," but only in the context of the dealership lot with a single sales objective.

Office environments can be too loaded with personality, ambitions, and a requirement for intimacy with those in charge. Those overwhelmed can be effectively treated if the other criterion of ADHD symptoms and an ADHD school history supports findings of this Decisive ADHD pattern.

These Decisive ADHD individuals, because they have been compensating for the abundant Thinking ADHD problems, simply can't adjust. In the modern corporate world, similar successful individuals often ask for a demotion to a previous level, or they can become depressed and crash dramatically.

They also may appear to others as "avoidant" and inappropriately perplexed by their new challenges. Often, they will unwittingly undo themselves by crossing a boundary within the organization. Rather than face their disappointments and their hidden Thinking handicap, they either leave or are asked to leave. They feel stupid, and can't stand the suggestion that they might be.

Freud suggested these victims of success fall apart upon achieving an "unconscious Oedipal victory," overcome with underlying guilt for winning. From a systems point of view, there may be some psychological truth in his observation. Guilt and conflict over winning may be a part of the problem.

In my experience, the history of ADHD with many of these presentations is striking, and "careful ADHD compensation over time" is often successful until the demands of being successful swamps Thinking ADHD types. In that new reality context, those with Thinking ADHD often fragment, and can fall apart in a cloud of maybes.

Chapter 5
Avoiding ADHD:
Not Thinking & Not Acting

Quality is everyone's responsibility.

W. Edwards Deming, Management Consultant

Tom suffers with more than social anxiety; he is a hermit and a hobo, a nomad without connections. Avoidance for Tom means not having to think, not having to worry about the details. He would rather be alone than deal with close relationships, with groups, or with specific work projects. Avoiding reality is another way of coping with reality, but becomes counterproductive over time. The solace with practicing avoidance is that one simply doesn't have to do anything, or think anything. They simply avoid the unmanageable variables by avoiding reality.

These people are stuck in time, often for a lifetime.

The "Not Thinking and Not Acting" subset looks like "avoidant personality." It is often associated with a clear history of ADHD and is the least frequently recognized subset of all three ADHD subsets. This type often appears as an Axis II/personality/character[17] problem, free from obvious conflict, often associated with having a big problem with authority. If you suffer with this subset, it will be difficult to responsibly seek help. You just don't want to go there. "Nope! Not me!"

Some with Avoiding ADHD demonstrate all four of the Avoidant subsets that I will discuss in a moment in their history; some compensate and only avoid the possibility of unstructured work in the context of a controlled, structured, isolated and avoidant home life. Some do well alone with themselves and close relationships, or with crowds and people, but in the end they simply can't deal with specific projects. Precise questions will set precise objectives to correct this subset.

These individuals often don't want any evaluation, don't want to talk, and are most comfortable at home in front of the TV. They often show a kind of surly, contemptuous disposition and an abiding disrespect for authority. They do not want to answer to anyone for anything. They resist psychiatric evaluation and resent any "psychobabble" during the evaluation, especially open-ended questions. It all involved too much thinking. They often suffer from an associated cognitive depression and

---

17 "Character" appears as without conflict, looking as if they choose to have that coping strategy, and are accused of having an "attitude."

vehemently deny affective depression.

They are frequently antisocial and don't want ongoing close relationships. Answering questions corrupts their mind-state of identity as a hobo, a hermit or a long-haul truck driver. Their mantra: "Just leave me alone." They suffer an obvious inability to participate in ordinary conversation. Their behavior is avoidant of any unknown entity and is associated with significant procrastination on any complex variables. They often don't look like they have an avoidant problem with projects, because they sincerely plan to get it done. "I will do it in just a minute ...give me a break." They resist change with a passion.

I had one patient who lived the life of a hermit and inherited a large trust fund, enough to buy a full city block in a busy tourist town. I pointed out to him that he clearly suffered from Avoiding ADHD and confirmed ADHD by guessing his entire school career without a hint of prior history from him. Not until he spent a day thinking about where to put a sign for parking did he recognize he was thinking way too much.

After years of isolation and a failure to recognize these problems -- and after previous multiple trials of SSRI meds -- he also arrived at an impasse on medication treatment. Every remote possible side effect he read about placed him into a deeper defensive, avoidant conflict, which he could not resolve. Had his condition been identified as a youth he could have been started on a full recovery path with medical intervention.

Treatment for ADHD would have turned him around as it has for many others, but as is often typical with Avoiding ADHD, he just couldn't decide on the medication issue, so he avoided the decision and the treatment. Years later he came back to confirm that I was right in my assessment, but still could not make an acceptable treatment decision -- stuck forever in avoidance.

These Avoiding ADHD folks may appear well engaged with society and the real world, but simply can't deal with projects. On the other hand, many do suffer with all four of these subsets and become either hermits or nomads, disconnected at every level of interpersonal activity, from self-reflection to projects, and drift along as a way of avoiding these different layers of changing reality.

The Four Subsets of Avoiding ADHD:
1. Avoidance of Self:

They disparage and refuse any self-reflection. Interestingly, some think self-reflection is counterproductive. Thinking more deeply about one's own problems, one's own misgivings, one's own mistakes, one's own life challenges often brings an associated complexity of considerations that feels insurmountable. There's no self-reflection and repetition of the same old problems. They absolutely refuse to consider thinking about thinking –- and as a result refuse any metacognitive[18] process.

Part of the problem: they don't want to admit they're wrong, or that they created a problem for others. Often, these individuals are on a rescue mission for the family and the world.

---

18 Metacognition: Self-reflection, a cognitive/thinking process necessary for recovery from ADHD thinking patterns.

They have no time for the self with all of that responsibility for fixing the world. They have the feeling: "I'm right, you're wrong, no need to reflect on that fact. And, by the way, I am saving the world; what the heck are you doing?"

These folks often function as seriously controlling managers, precisionists and perfectionists, trying to avoid any whining or indication of difficulty. They often come into treatment with a loved one who simply insists they seek help, and, of course, ADHD is not even remotely on their radar. Because they haven't considered ADHD, they may simply not get over the shock of that new diagnosis -- after all, they "aren't hyper."

2. Avoidance of Close Relationships: Intimacy

As personal relationships become more intimate over time, the Avoidant must withdraw. As they become closer to another on any one of several levels of intimacy[19], they are overcome with the complexity of new variables. From the intimacy of gossip and clichés, to physical or sexual intimacy, each level requires more self-sufficiency and greater self-knowledge. With greater personal intimacy, they face increasing multiple variables. Discussions about feelings are far too imprecise.

Your space, your essence, who you are, changes with close relationships. Growing numbers of boundary questions require clearer understandings of self, and of self-awareness. These individuals are also often micromanagers, can't deal with the complexity of group opinion, and keep a critical, negative eye on operations at the office. "Team" concepts and behaviors are too threatening.

---

19 Kelly, M, *The Seven Levels of Intimacy: The Art of Loving and the Joy of Being Loved*, Fireside: 2005.

Described by de Bono in *Six Thinking Hats*,[20] these are often the negative "Black Hat" crowd, always struggling to keep their cognitive distance by dismissing Green Hat thinking. Green Hat means possible change, and they do not want change; they love the negative because negativity prevents change.

Executive coaches[21] recognize these controlling, counterproductive cognitive patterns as one of the most important challenges in their consultation practices. The successful avoidant Black Hats can be quite seductive in person, but you never feel you can trust them, as they never can reveal themselves to others. Imperfection is intolerable in self or others. So they remain alone.

3. Avoidance of Groups or People in General:

Group and social relationships are avoided. Group intimacy introduces different cognitive variables than personal intimacy. Additional people add more unpredictable variables, more possibilities to think about. Just small talk can demand more thinking. More people in your environment can prompt more worry about what others are thinking. Many with this set of problems do well with spouses, but simply can't cope in the broader world.

Social intimacies, teamwork, groups, meetings, parties, talking on the telephone may all trigger avoidance. This subset of ADHD-challenged individuals is often misidentified as suffering with social anxiety, and they are treated with, you guessed it, SSRIs, which make this type of problem worse over time. They may help in the short run, but often deteriorate in

20 de Bono, E. *Six Thinking Hats*, Back Bay Books, 1999, 2nd Ed.
21 Fitzgerald, C. and Garvey-Berger, J. *Executive Coaching: Practices and Perspectives*, Davies-Black, 2002.

effectiveness over several weeks or months as thinking abilities deteriorate.

Vertical managers[22] with their personal view of the world inflicted on the "family," keep the parental attitude, and treat colleagues like errant children. Team considerations? Adult to adult communications? Forget it -- way too many variables. I'm the boss.

4. Project Avoidance:

Required projects meet with procrastination. Project Avoidance is subtle and may occur only in the family context. Often those suffering with this subset do well for specific periods. They are good at work, listen in school, but simply can't pitch in around the home, can't do homework and don't work well outside of specifically structured obligations.

Remember, there are two forms of procrastination: starting and finishing. These project-avoidant types often look like they don't have an ADHD problem in the context of some structure, but key responsibilities in the context of unstructured settings often go undone, or suffer significant delay. An interesting characteristic of these folks is that they can often become workaholics because they create a structure at work that is predictable. They know that work reality; they often control that reality and simply don't want to deal with the unpredictable quality of new, unfamiliar tasks with possible criticism.

Some workaholics become emotionally entangled with a work assistant who does what he says in the office, and he may leave his spouse to enjoy the apparent security and control that comes with that new relationship. Vertical management

22 Manage from the top down with the clear message that they control everything.

works at work, but not at home. You guessed it: out of the work environment, the control is gone, the same problems prevail with the assistant away from work, and he feels abandoned and alone. All he wants to do: keep the structure, to keep the control.

Avoiding ADHD Summary

Avoiding ADHD is the hardest subset to diagnosis because these folks in this grouping are in denial due to their avoidance. They can look very much like bums, hermits or the lone cowboy, The Stranger in *High Plains Drifter* or the Clint character in *Gran Torino*. They don't need a shrink -- don't need anyone. Both thinking and acting become problematic, so it is easier to remain frozen in time, not to think or do anything. They are not reflective, but avoidant; not deep, but trying to stay shallow and purely cognitive and operational, thereby diminishing emotion and unpredictable feelings.

And, as you may have guessed, these folks do not want therapy, don't want to talk, and don't want to think about anything ambiguous. While they are often quite intelligent, they often seek repetitive jobs such as working on an assembly line. Marriage is almost impossible when all four avoidant subsets are present, unless the spouse wishes to remain a victim, or is completely avoidant as well.

Remember, Avoiding ADHD demonstrates several symptoms at different times. Yes, most of us avoid some aspects of reality, but most often we buckle down and do it. It's essential to understand context, to understand how the brain works in different realities or settings.

Those with Avoiding ADHD don't move ahead as they should. They aren't lazy, though they may say they are. They just can't cognitively take those next functional brain steps. They want to live with their parents.

This presentation has huge implications for those in human resources who consistently wonder why that excellent person just couldn't succeed at the next level of responsibility. My experience is that if this characteristic of Avoiding ADHD is correctly identified the person can advance -- and succeed -- at work. But this ADHD condition must remain top secret, as others knowing of the problem will frequently shame them with ADHD gossip into a depressed, regressive, failure state.

Summary For Your Evolved Diagnostic Thinking

Think brain function, not appearances, and put aside the hyperactive and inattentive debate before your first visit with the doctor. Seek specific treatment objectives: ADHD treatment should address the cause of the ADHD symptoms, whatever the surface description, and will be quite different depending upon associated comorbid conditions.

Treatment does not differ based upon descriptive ADHD subsets. Treatment does differ based on understanding of the deeper functional findings.

Communicate these functional findings and objectives to the doctor as soon as you understand the implications.

The medication management will align with the precision of the diagnosis. Precise diagnosis, achieved through cooperation of all interested parties, will help with precise medication strategies.

From the physician's point of view, the science of diagnosis and medication management strategies must be introduced from the outset of the interview to dispel any feelings that doctors simply don't know what they are doing.

The prefrontal cortex deals with thinking and acting and some irritable emotional imbalances. Starting with thinking and acting will set markers for mutual understanding with your medical team.

These three functional ADHD presentations and their subsets build measurable office objectives. If the diagnosis is measurable in the office, and the medications have measurable delivery systems, the science then makes outcomes more predictable.

By asking questions of children, and engaging them in the entire process at every meeting, communication builds the child's self-assessment, self-esteem and self-mastery.

When other, more challenging interventions arise, and if medications prove unpredictable, the entire treatment team should respond with feedback and improved, perhaps biomedical, measurement strategies.

Chapter 6
Measure Metabolism:
The Burn Rate

Everything should be as simple as it is,
but not simpler.

Albert Einstein

Mandy has been taking stimulant medications for ADHD since she was in junior high, and now she is a mother with two kids. She has never been able to find out why the medications seem to work for a while and then lose their effectiveness over time. After multiple changes over many years she consulted with me to discover she suffered with a specific gluten sensitivity that corrupted her bowel, her liver and her metabolic rate with those different medications. The changes came from her gut disrepair, not from her stress in life. She thought she was simply untreatable.

Mandy's gut is only one of the many burn rate variables at play in any medication management strategy. Burn rate changes require adjustments to dosage and ADHD dosing strategies.

Stimulant medications for ADHD behave in predictable ways. Just as we test the soil in organic gardening, we can test both brain and body health. If your body doesn't work correctly the stimulant medications or the supplements you take won't work correctly either. If you don't know the multiple factors that can modify burn rate you will almost always blame yourself for problems with medications. This chapter cannot possibly cover all the variables that can affect the rate of medication metabolism, but I will outline some of the basics so you can begin to consider different alternatives with your medical team.

If you don't have a clue how ADHD medications work, how they "burn" in your body, you won't know what to expect with treatment.

This chapter will make metabolic rate inquiries part of your fact-finding mission.

Basic burn rate awareness, more than any single piece of information, can make or break any medication treatment. After that initial diagnosis -- as you start to consider medications -- you must not approach treatment without some fundamental appreciation of burn rate variations. And if you get this simple metabolic point, you can save yourself years of medication confusion and problems.

Without information about metabolic variations, you won't know how to measure the medication effectiveness during treatment. Secondly, the overall treatment process will appear considerably less predictable. You will become confused. The meds just won't work right, and you'll likely also become very frustrated. Many simply quit treatment and continue to suffer the developmental stasis of ADHD because they don't appreciate the simplicity of these burn rate rules.

Brain And Body Misunderstandings

Remember, the brain is not like Mount Everest sitting up in the crystal clear, unpolluted snow above the clouds, upstream where the rivers start. On the contrary, our brains live at the other end of our body's burning debris in the brain swamp, the end point of all of our body's poorly metabolized rubbish. It spins there in the swill of whatever is broken or rusty in your metabolic pathways, from bowel to gut to liver to kidneys. Think for a moment of the metabolic flotsam that drifts downstream from the trash we all eat. Then take a moment to consider how metabolism affects your thinking brain.

Your brain is the canary in the coal mine for associated chronic biomedical imbalances. If your metabolism is off, if you suffer from immune, autoimmune, or other chronic medical conditions, your brain will very likely react to those underlying conditions.

Burn rate is an approximate measure of how healthy or rusty your body is, even before you start ADHD medications. The simple outcome of slowed and faulty metabolism is slowed burning of your medications. If you are slow in your metabolism you will be slow at burning medications, and you will likely need a lower than expected dose. Dosage of medication should be directly related to these predictable burn rate variables. This metabolic burn rate perspective is so fundamentally useful, it's amazing that it's so consistently overlooked.

Using this concept with drug dosage at first sounds a bit complicated, but burn rate is easy to assess. While not always completely accurate, the simple medical guidelines in this chapter will encourage more mindfulness and deliberate use of medications, with far fewer side effects. Most often, just knowing these metabolic possibilities often significantly influences treatment and encourages a more conservative, lower-dosage strategy.

Causes of Burn Rate Problems

The most common cause of variation in burn rates is underlying poor metabolism, which creates an accumulation of drugs, resulting in a feeling of overdosage. These unpredictable problems are found repeatedly, and they significantly affect the outcome of using stimulant drugs to treat ADHD.

To explain the problem more completely, these often overlooked metabolic, functional body issues will significantly change the metabolism of ADHD medications. They often create significant secondary emotional and cognitive problems that can destroy treatment objectives.These metabolic barriers often block the somatic breakdown of the medication, rendering ADHD medications ineffective (less often, requiring more dosage than expected to create a clinical effect), or most often, prevent or slow their metabolic assimilation, thereby creating a state of relative toxicity wherein the medications appear too high in dosage because they are accumulating rather than undergoing appropriate metabolic burning, and elimination.

If the burn rate is impaired, the rate of metabolism is impaired, the drain is broken or rusty, and the medications accumulate and the sink will stop up. An emotionally or cognitively flooded bathroom can result in significant medication reaction problems as listed below.

Bear in mind that these following burn rate changes are not listed in a specific order of prevalence, but occur so often they should be on everyone's clinical radar.

Gut Problems Secondary To Allergies:

One of the most frequently missed issues in current psychiatric office practice is food allergies and food intolerances. For example, allergies or sensitivities to gluten (wheat protein) and casein (milk protein) present undetected problems for many people.

The GI tract, about the size of a singles tennis court when all stretched out in adults, is the largest detoxification and immunity management system in your body. On the one hand, it brings in nutrients; on the other hand, it rids the body of waste. As the primary sewage treatment plant in your body, it needs care and attention.

If your bowel is rusty or broken, slow or fast, the ADHD medications (and other psych medications in general) will not work as well. In fact, they will, over time, become predictably *ineffective*. Furthermore, as we often see from the laboratory assessment of many picky eaters (by using neurotransmitter biomarker evaluations), the neurotransmitters may simply exist in such deficiency that nothing works, no matter what you do.

All psych meds collect neurotransmitters; they *don't add neurotransmitters*. To add neurotransmitters we must add neurotransmitter precursors to the mix. But even the neurotransmitter precursor supplements don't work if the bowel is corrupted by allergic reactions.

Without serotonin, without dopamine, without norepinephrine, just what exists in the synapse for the selective re-uptake inhibitors to inhibit? You can't prevent re-uptake if nothing is there to re-uptake in the first place. This is basic.

So why don't we ask that basic functional bowel question more carefully on the front end?

"Number Two" Achieves New Target Status!

With every new patient, I always ask this simple question: "How many times a day do you go Number Two?" I've come a long way from my life as a '70s psychoanalyst in Philadelphia where the most important questions were, "What are your dreams?" and "What are your fantasies?" In contemporary psychiatry, using medications for treatment, judging biologic variables and measuring metabolic rates for the medications will significantly improve medication predictability. And, no, this focus isn't just anal. I always ask every new patient about both the north (upper GI) and the south (Number Two) activities of the gastrointestinal tract!

We live in a more biologic world than we could ever appreciate in the 1970s. Today, antigens/immunity must be on the radar, or we'll miss the target.

Many gut/bowel problems can affect the rate of metabolism. To repeat: metabolism always effects dosage.

Let's start with an example of gluten sensitivity. With

an allergy/sensitivity to wheat/gluten, the patient's bowel movement frequency can linger either below one bowel movement a day or go up to more than three movements a day. I've had patients confess that they have been irregular since childhood, with a history of depression and ADHD, and been resistant to psychiatric meds for years. Not surprisingly, the medications work for a while and then lose their effectiveness. When the bowel and allergies are corrected, medications not only work consistently over time, but also often require lower doses.

This essential rule in ADHD treatment: Dosage matters! Exact dosage matters even more.

Doesn't the process of measuring/asking about bowel problems make sense if we are working to correct the dosage?

Ask Yourself About Transit Time

In some suburban quarters, "transit time" refers to the length of the commute to work. At medical conferences, "transit time" refers to the length of the "commute" of "food intake" to "food output" down south. A healthy time for a good bowel transit is eighteen to twenty-four hours. Shorter or longer transit times can create problems. I regularly see patients with forty-eight-hour transit times, and have intervened on one person with more than twenty-one days of transit time. Her transit time was slower than a crosstown bus. She had told many previous physicians that she had "a problem with constipation," but no one chased down the details. No, I won't tell you here about the extensive details of that tri-weekly monolithic stool delivery. Think: hours -- and pain.

And, in case you wondered, she looked very bipolar on meds

until we corrected the underlying food allergy by significantly limiting her diet.

You don't need expensive X-rays or refined substances to measure your transit time. Simply measure that metabolic marker by eating a good meal of highly "visible" foods, such as corn or beets. Measure/count the transit time:[23] hours from the mouth to the south, and voila! -- transit time becomes a workable number, a metabolic target. Your recovery target: about once a day, formed and connected stools; less than one per day, too slow, more than three per day, going to the too-many side.

Even subtle irregularity often occurs from childhood and birth. Sensitivity can be inherited and begin during intrauterine development. Some are born with GI symptoms and can significantly jeopardize brain function. And remember, "silent celiac"[24] problems that significantly affect neurologic/brain functions often occur without specific frequency changes in BM activity, yet the neurologic problems persist in spite of no overt GI[25] symptoms.

If a person has bowel issues, remember that most GI specialists are looking for advanced/true Celiac Disorder[26] with serious bowel pathology, seen on a biopsy. The subtle, chronic metabolic effect of these less-obvious symptomatic bowel allergies/allergens, as seen with gluten or casein sensitivity, is often overlooked, and is sometimes outright disputed. They're focused on gut pathology; we're focused on the brain.

Gluten (a wheat protein), and casein (a milk protein), sensitivity can significantly contribute to many psychiatric

23 Transit Time measurement outlined - 1 page, http://bit.ly/ttnew
24 New England Journal of Medicine Editorial on Silent Celiac
25 U of Chicago: http://www.uchicagokidshospital.org/pdf/uch_007934.pdf
26 Hoggan: Gluten Sensitivity and Celiac Differentiated celiac.com

presentations and significantly affect medication interventions for ADHD. Depression and ADHD often reside downstream from these metabolic problems, aggravated by associated malnutrition and multiple deficiencies.

More Than Simple Wheat Or Milk Allergies

In addition to gluten and casein sensitivity, many additional allergens can trigger ADHD symptoms and include garlic, soy, peanuts, and eggs. Further, these additional antigens can create very significant life problems, from appearing bipolar, to depression, to ongoing anxiety, especially in those with predominant somatic features such as IBS-Irritable Bowel Syndrome and Crohn's.

Patients with resistant, complex ADHD problems who don't respond to medical treatment often have significant problems with reactions to a variety of allergens. Their medications just don't work right. If your exhausted bowel has a kind of chronic poison ivy inside lining the bowel wall, how can it work right? If you look at the cross sections of the slides of those bowels, the villi are almost completely gone. No villi results in significant malabsorption, leaky gut, and significant immune reactions that can look like ADHD, depression, anxiety or bipolar disorder.

Chicken And Egg Testing

Stimulant medications don't treat food allergies. Testing for IgG antibodies for food sensitivity is a useful way to start, and the labs in the back of this book have that testing available.

A Clue To Burn Rate

One of the easiest ways to measure burn rate is by considering objective assessment of the Therapeutic Window.[27] Make the Therapeutic Window your new best friend. The Therapeutic Window will keep the medical team on target as it assesses treatment objectives and medication predictability.

Too often, stimulant drugs are adjusted incorrectly. It may appear as though the drug is working, but the dose is actually inadequate. In our offices we have for years measured DOE (duration of effectiveness) at every medication check, and doing so inevitably provides measurable, correctable information.

Metabolic rate will determine the DOE with these shorter (less than 24 hours) half-life medications. The history of stimulant medications has for years focused on lengthening the half-life with longer acting, time-release agents. "Half-life" is synonymous with the expected DOE. Burn rate will modify how the half-life appears based on that specific individual's unique metabolism.

Who can know if they are working correctly without using specific markers and a more specific medication measurement process? And if you don't know, are you supposed to guess? Such imprecise, ambiguous questions are medically useless. Yet the oversight of ignoring these measures is common in the medical community. Without that information it's almost impossible to adjust dosages correctly for each person.

Liver Problems And The Therapeutic Window

If any bowel issues are present, the liver often begins to compensate for the difficulties, even though actual liver function

27 Therapeutic Window http://bit.ly/txwindow

values may not reveal the change. If the liver is compromised with these additional metabolic pressures, then the metabolic rate for medications changes and the meds don't work as expected.

The Bulletproof Liver

Patients can develop what seems like a bulletproof liver, meaning the meds do not metabolize effectively. Medications seem to literally bounce off, immediately or months after starting. It's like they aren't taking meds at all, or as noted above, multiple attempts to manipulate the ADHD meds simply don't work.

Stimulant medications and almost all psychiatric meds are first metabolized primarily in the liver. If the specific medications are not adequately metabolized, they can accumulate and cause toxic reactions. Even small doses can appear to present as an overdose. Liver challenges slow the metabolic rate, which can shrink, or narrow, the Therapeutic Window. The result: a small increase in meds becomes too much and a slight adjustment downward proves inadequate. No one, including myself, can hit that narrow sweet spot, because it's simply metabolically impossible.

I have seen cases where the labs "all look good, WNL (Within Normal Limits)," and have later discovered that the liver is actually functioning metabolically as bulletproof. You as a patient, you as a medical professional, will ultimately discover these problems if you keep this basic tenant in mind: if the medications don't work as expected, trace backwards. If you find yourself repeatedly chasing the effective Therapeutic Window, metabolic problems almost certainly are erecting barriers to your anticipated positive outcome.

Over time and trials, you will ultimately find yourself reflecting and backtracking on what appears to be remarkable, unpredictable and refractory medical sensitivity, with no progress on any meds. Those on the receiving end of this frequent problem feel frustrated and incurable. They actually are incurable, until this underlying imbalanced predicament is corrected.

Heavy Metal Toxicity

Heavy metals such as lead and mercury can manifest as ADHD. Routine blood testing alone may not reveal heavy metal issues, but simple blood/serum screening can provide clues, and should be encouraged, and hair analysis can prove even more beneficial. Urine tests also can help a doctor detect heavy metal toxins. And once discovered, practitioners can chelate (remove) toxic elements from patients. Many of our Defeat Autism Now[28] doctors have known for years how to detoxify carefully without adding addition medical problems. If detoxification is necessary it can prove lifesaving in the face of futility and ambiguous results.

Hormone Imbalance

Hormone-related problems with some individuals start before puberty. Measurement is not difficult and provides useful evidence that can be used to make medication and treatment adjustments. ADHD meds do not work as a treatment for hormone problems such as Graves' disease or polycystic ovaries.

Very frequently middle-aged women suffer from estrogen

---

28 DAN link: http://www.defeatautismnow.com

dominance and symptomatically appear as ADHD, yet have very significant hormonal/metabolic issues from adolescence that stimulant meds can appear to correct in the short run. But often those stimulant medications will prove ineffective in the long run based upon the associated hormonal issues. Remember that significant immune dysfunction, as already noted, can begin during an intrauterine experience, and that hormone dysfunction often occurs in childhood, is often associated with poor diet, an early or late onset of menses, and is often associated with chronic gastrointestinal issues.

Essential Drug-to-Drug Interactions

Drug interactions are like the old problem of cigarette smoking and lung cancer. Just because some incorrectly assert that the correlation isn't in the current literature doesn't mean it doesn't exist. They are simply reading the wrong literature, or not reading the literature at all. These non-believers simply haven't used sufficient magnification in their offices to see the real details. Drug interactions are not a belief system. They exist as demonstrable clinical facts. If you know about them, you can save yourself considerable difficulties.

Some uninformed professionals even recommend using *known negative drug interactions* to modify medications dosage. Drug-interaction researchers debunk this capricious and incorrect suggestion and advice against this practice. If drugs are interacting, the interaction is itself unpredictable in rate, occurring sometimes six months down the treatment road. This causes long-term unpredictable, even toxic, drug-to-drug outcomes that can harm patients and families. I have witnessed the effects of this unwise practice after years of patients being placed incorrectly on the wrong mix of medications, for the wrong reasons, yet with the right diagnosis.

Wrong meds, wrong dosage titration,[29] ignored interaction, will guarantee significant problems that are often identified as bipolar disorder.

One person came to my office after their psychiatrist pontificated, "These drug interactions are not a problem. In fact, you can use Prozac to lower your dosage of Adderall XR. Prozac blocks Adderall, and we can then increase the half-life of the Adderall, meaning you can use a smaller dose of Adderall!" They came in for a second opinion after years of ineffective cognition, inadequate focus, toxic feelings and dangerous rages on Adderall. Simple solution: Change the antidepressant, not the Adderall itself. Outcome: Adderall proved predictably effective after the dosage was correctly adjusted.

Drug interactions can make a person crazy, especially if mixing stimulant medications with drugs that slow or significantly interfere with their metabolism. If anyone's plumbing is plugged with interactions, just as it is with bowel challenges, the stimulant drugs build up and create toxic reactions. This sounds basic, but many continue to ignore the implications of these extensively researched, commonly witnessed problems.

Drug-to-drug interactions are not debatable. They are reported throughout the literature, but are simply not registered on many practitioners' radar. The big reason these interactions are ignored is that they are subtle and occur over time, *appearing to be unrelated* to the changes months ago. If you need a reference, I regularly use this important interaction

29 Titration: going slowly up in dosage

book: *Drug Interaction Principles For Medical Practice.*[30]

Burn Rate Symptoms From Drug-to-Drug Interactions

Patients Look Overdosed: Drug-to-drug interactions appear as a stimulant medication overdose. If the patient is taking amphetamines, the toxicity reaction is hyper-focused, angry, and irritable. If methylphenidates are overdosed, the most frequent toxic reaction is the feeling "stoned." I have seen many who behaved psychotically on both of these types of meds when overdosed.

Interactions Are Often Later: Drug interactions are often subtle and appear chronically, over time, not immediately as one might expect. Drug interactions with stimulants often don't show themselves in the first week or two because the blockage of one drug by the other is often incomplete.

Drug Trials Don't Assess Interactions: Often drug trials, either in the safety or efficacy stages of research for FDA approval, don't take into account metabolic pathways. In fact, many studies exclude those with possible interactions. Neither the FDA nor pharmaceutical companies want to evaluate interactions if they are simply seeking efficacy and safety confirmation. Since drug interactions with ADHD medications frequently don't appear immediately, they are repeatedly overlooked in initial safety studies.

---

30 Wynn, G, Cozza K, Armstrong S, Osterheld J, *Drug Interaction Principles for Medical Practice*, Amer. Psychiatric Assoc Press, 1st Ed 2008

Limit Drug Interaction Surprises: Look for drug interactions such as those listed below any time from the start of medications to six-to-eight months after the first prescription is written. Drug interactions won't be a surprise if you predict them, anticipate them and engage the whole team in that watchful process.

How Drug Interactions Occur In The First Place

The Blocking Mechanism: One medication, (an inhibitor/blocker) actively blocks the metabolism of another (called a substrate), which is passively coming up through a specific enzyme pathway or pipeline. Each pipeline has a specific name, and they are well identified in the literature. When the blocker inhibits the substrate, the drug going through that pipeline backs up, like the sink in the bathroom. The backup accumulates and becomes toxic, leaving the patient feeling like they are out of control.

Frequent Blocking Example: Prozac and Paxil significantly block one of the two most important pathways in the liver for many psychiatric drugs, especially Dexedrine, Adderall, and Vyvanse. If the pathway is blocked, the drug that passes through that pipeline backs up, increases in intensity and can actually make the patient psychotic on the resulting toxic reaction. This toxicity, with symptoms ranging from feeling jittery to paranoia, is common if taken together.

Stimulant Drug-Drug Interactions: Dexedrine, Adderall and Vyvanse are all amphetamines. The liver and kidneys metabolize them, and the first pass is through that enzyme-system pipeline. If that 2D6 pipe is blocked by Prozac or Paxil, amphetamines accumulate, with resultant anger, rage, mind racing, sleep deprivation and subsequent lack of control, even associated with paranoia. As I noted above, the mild interactions can look like the medications need adjusting, appearing as if the ADHD has returned full force, as the patient pops out the top of the Therapeutic Window. Now that both Prozac and Paxil are generic drugs, they are prescribed even more frequently to those with insurance limitations. Paxil, Prozac and amphetamine/stimulant reaction is on the rise, yet still under the radar for many. Depression is the most frequent comorbid problem with ADHD, and this predictable drug interaction is one of the most common.

Which Drug Caused Which Reaction: Since these reactions occur often months after starting treatment, the stimulant often inappropriately takes the blame. The stimulant and the ADHD diagnosis already have a bad reputation. Drug-to-drug interactions such as these place the use of stimulants, the diagnosis of ADHD and the whole ADHD intervention process in a costly, disappointing and often infuriating inconsistency. No wonder ADHD diagnosis and treatment is so often considered ridiculous. In this case, however, the antidepressant is the bad guy. And the problem is so easy to fix.

Do "Wash Out The Prozac:" Prozac has a half-life of weeks, not days and is stored in the brain fat. If a person has been taking Prozac for years and is diagnosed with ADHD, and the practitioner would like to start an amphetamine, take time to first wash out the Prozac. Don't start the amphetamine until at least a week after stopping the Prozac, because a backup is much more likely with a brain full of blocker trash. I never use Prozac or Paxil with amphetamine stimulants for these reasons.

Genetic Variation With The Burn Rate: The old rule that stimulant drugs should be given according to body weight is very old news. Stimulant metabolic rates are markedly idiosyncratic in their metabolic rates. Many small people need larger doses, and many larger patients arrive at my office uniformly overdosed, just because of their size. The big guys were started too high, and kept too high for the many years they have been taking meds because the practitioner didn't consider metabolism but instead relied on weight as a mitigating variable. New technology has helped us understand even more about these metabolic pathways.

The Big CYP 450 Pipes: Some pipes are exceedingly big, and the burn rate is very fast, so more drugs are needed to work effectively. These are the hardest to adjust, as the meds appear ineffective until you reach an action threshold. This rate requires off-label dosing, not FDA approved doses. Beware: fast-burn rate can occur with other metabolic irregularities, and often does.

The Impossible Pipes: Some are so small they genetically interfere with any drug passing through. Seven- to ten-percent of Caucasians, and three percent of African-Americans, lack a certain pathway, significantly limiting the burn rate, and creating a toxic reaction soon after starting even on a very low dose of an amphetamine stimulant.

The Average Pipes: Less than half of the population has an average rate of metabolism. This fact alone encourages a low and slow intervention process, and no cookie-cutter dosing strategies, ever: "Take this dose, then take this, then stop when you feel like you've gone too far" is simply not an acceptable titration strategy.

The Narrow Pipes: These 2D6 systems are very narrow, and will accumulate quickly if the dosage is increased too rapidly. This finding alone is enough to discourage those who use fixed strategies over the first three-to-four weeks without carefully watching the patient. Toxic reactions occur with too-rapid dosage increases.

On a final important note regarding these CYP pathways and the clinical usefulness of genetics with both receptors and re-uptake inhibitors: these sites are all measureable now, and in our practice we more routinely measure these exceedingly common challenges with a simple saliva sample from the mouth.

How To: Burn Rate Awareness - Specific DOEs

Go low and slow. No cookie-cutter dose changing strategies; only a custom titration for every patient.

Plan to use your new knowledge to think about these built-in metabolic variables so that you can predict better outcomes.

Remember the genetics, the drug interaction possibilities, the bowel and the allergic challenges that can all change the burn rate, and then correct the correctable. Offending allergens require their own protocols for recovery.

Spread the word on the Prozac and Paxil interaction. It's all over the place, but avoidable with several antidepressants that don't significantly block 2D6. Specific clean 2D6 antidepressants are: Pristiq, Effexor, Lexapro, Celexa, Luvox and Zoloft -- these qualify for minimal interactions on 2D6. Wellbutrin and Cymbalta show moderate inhibition of 2D6, and at higher doses of those antidepressants expect the possibility of 2D6 interactions.

Remember breakfast. It will help with the assimilation of stimulant medications. See the chapter here on breakfast.

If neurotransmitters are low, as they always are in picky eaters, then stimulant interventions for ADHD often simply don't work. The bowel and brain are so far behind that it may take months to build a sufficient foundation of neurotransmitters. Measure neurotransmitters first.

Multiple diagnoses require carefully adjusted multiple medications.

Complex problems require more metabolic review and a better look at neurotransmitter biomarkers. This testing is paid by most insurance.

Discuss DOE and the Therapeutic Window at every medication check.

Each psychiatric medication requires its own dosage strategy, its own characteristic metabolic signature.

Watch carefully at the outset for the DOE to maximize the dose for best effectiveness.

Each drug must be dialed in for the expected DOE. The dosage is then determined by the DOE meeting the expected time. Dosage is not determined by weight, age, sex, or simply globally reporting "it's working."

Targets: When the dosage is correct, these are target times we look for and expect for best efficacy.

    Ritalin immediate release (IR) – four hours

    Ritalin extended release (XR) – eight hours

    Concerta (an XR) – eight to nine hours

    Adderall IR – five to six hours

    Adderall XR – eight to ten hours

    Dexedrine IR – five hours

    Dexedrine XR – seven hours

    Metadate CR (XR) - eight hours

    Focalin IR – four hours

    Focalin XR – eight to nine hours

    Daytrana Patch - ten to twelve hours

    Vyvanse (XR)- adults twelve to fourteen hours[31] - children ten to twelve hours

Insufficient dosage causes less effective/shorter DOE across all medications.

The most effective medications last all day, covering the late evening.

Compliance in the late afternoon drops when adding another IR dose, leaving the evening disorganized and troubled.

---

31 Vyvanse Titration Link And Video: http://bit.ly/doetitrate

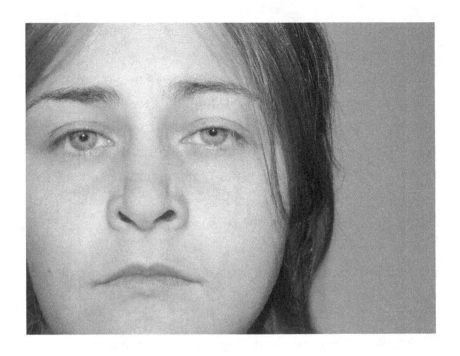

Chapter 7
Depression & Anxiety:
ADHD Confusion

*It is not enough to do your best; you must
know what to do, and then do your best.*

W. Edwards Deming, Management Consultant

Depression is, without a doubt, one of the most dangerous conditions when combined with ADHD. Depression increases if it co-exists with ADHD and you treat only the ADHD. If you do miss it, you have big problems, like suicidal thinking. I know I've said it before -- it bears repeating: Your medications could be significantly mixed up.

Everything I am about to tell you comes not only from my research, my brain imaging work and my office experience, but from real experience in the field, out across the country visiting hundreds of other child and adult psychiatrists, pediatricians, family practitioners, internists, nurse practitioners and physicians assistants. Their collective experience numbers in the many thousands of patient hours and deserves attention. That on-the-road experience and those scores of discussions all around the country affirm my own understanding of depression and ADHD.

Medical Progress And Depression Treatment

Let's face the facts. Many doctors write for psychiatric medications without formal training in psychotropic medications. While many are comfortable with ADHD medications, they have significant hesitancy to write for antidepressant medications. Some reasons for the challenges with antidepressant medications are:

Information on neurophysiology has changed so dramatically in just the past few years that new cellular information seems quite unreal. Deep information, new languages, indeed new words, confound keeping up with the research in the labs, much less with clinical research.

SPECT, fMRI and other brain imaging systems can actually see where specific neurotransmitters become active in the brain. SPECT can help see variations in brain activity and helps with diagnostic challenges. While SPECT imaging is time consuming and expensive to learn, seeing the brain in action confirms these depression observations. But even today many without imaging experience remain unconvinced of the value of brain imaging - thus discouraging the use of SPECT evidence and, even more importantly, functional thinking.

Antidepressants have become increasingly more effective and more widely used, even for treating more than depression. But they have often been used without thinking. Many doctors feel uncomfortable making the diagnosis of depression. They worry about medical responsibility for a condition they don't fully understand. Writing for these medications carries significant legal implications, an increased concern for the marginally informed.

We know much more about the metabolic pathways and how they can and do interfere with certain medications causing drug-to-drug interactions. Drug interactions abound, and multiple drug treatments remain a challenge for the less informed.

The world of stimulant medications has changed even more profoundly, moving from first and second-generation stimulants to now a third- generation stimulant.

The trend toward using antipsychotics and mood stabilizers (e.g. Risperdal and Lithium) for emotional impulsivity has dramatically increased. Bipolar-mood disorder diagnosis is the current favorite wastebasket diagnosis, and is significantly on the rise, requiring multiple second opinions even from trained psychiatrists. The practice of more drugs for imprecise diagnoses based upon appearances is becoming commonplace, requiring more informed review.

The entire practice of treating ADHD with medications is now significantly altered by the encumbrance of ill-informed managed care companies that insist on short-acting stimulants that carry more risk for abuse, and are often more difficult to titrate. "Non-compliance" and ADHD are almost synonymous, but many in managed care nevertheless insist on short-acting stimulants that must be taken several times a day regardless of the obvious safety and compliance issues. Cost is regularly prioritized over patient safety and efficacy.

On the positive side of these matters, we can be much more confident regarding side effects and medication predictability than we were even five years ago. Mixing antidepressants with stimulants is possible and quite reasonable, if only you and your team are informed about possible challenges. But the challenges do require more time and attention.

So let's get back to the basics. First find the target, the correct diagnosis; then determine the specific medications. Depression at first seems easy, but even the "easy" depression is often missed, simply because few understand the significant relationship between depression and ADHD, especially using medications simultaneously.

First: Recognize The Two Forms Of Depression

Depression comes in two functional colors: thinking depression and feeling depression. Thinking (Cognitive) Depression is regularly overlooked with severe consequences. If the cognitive subset isn't identified or is treated only with stimulants, the results can become catastrophic. We aren't thinking enough about thinking as it applies to this depression finding.

So just how can you identify this "Thinking Depression?" Cognitive depression is an "I don't care" depression, while affective, emotional depression is an "I care too much" subset.

Depression And ADHD

We rarely, if ever, separate thinking depression from affective, emotional depression by appearances. ("If you don't look depressed, you probably aren't.") Often the cognitive aspect of depression, the apathy and indifference, is seen as the "I don't care" attitude –- understood as a personality disorder. Cognitive depression is not widely accepted as a serious problem in its own right.

My recommendation: always diagnostically break down the types of depression -- cognitive/thinking and affective/feeling. Ask yourself the apathy question to delineate possible depression.

Remember this important objective: No one should treat depression with ADHD medications, and ADHD medications do regularly make depression worse. Yes, cognitive depression may arise with ADHD, and may indeed be secondary, caused by the ADHD, or can exist as a separate, treatable problem. A dose of stimulant medications for those on the ADHD-depression seesaw often unwittingly leads to that too-frequent misdiagnoses: bipolar. And with that kind of bipolar diagnosis, based upon appearances, comes another host of inappropriate medications.

The bottom line: Recognize cognitive depression and preemptively deal with it.

Affective Depression:
Sadness, Whining And Vulnerability

Once you see the cognitive depression, the rest is easy. Whining, sadness, crying easily, having many problems with peers, vulnerability, all of these can appear independently or secondarily to ADHD. In any formulation of a treatment plan, the depression must be considered and the specific outcomes must be anticipated. If you don't predict these changes, they may become unpleasant surprises with an unexpected emotional price.

Depression By The Numbers: The Kelsey Scale

Use the Kelsey Scale to evaluate your own depression and keep track of its resolution. Dr. Jeff Kelsey was a friend of mine, and a psychiatric medical researcher at Emory University before he died a few years ago. Jeff attended Stanford, had a great tongue-in-cheek delivery and became a nationally recognized psychopharmacologist, forming his own research group in Atlanta. We had some great speaking opportunities together.

Jeff wrote a paper that used a simple scale from 1-10 to evaluate depression in the office, a difference from the then-commonly-used research standard for depression. Knowing that none of us in private practice had time to ask every question associated with that standard depression test –- the Hamilton Depression Inventory -- he created an easy way to validate clinical progress or deterioration with an easy question that statistically correlated with the standard depression test used for research.

The main Kelsey Scale question for this useful office evaluation, this convenient scale for depression measurement, is: "With 1 indicating the most severe, suicidal and completely depressed state, and 10 on the feeling great side (feeling like you're just getting off a plane in Paris), what is the number where you live on average?" This scale statistically related to the

HAM-D[32] as follows: 7 or higher correlated statistically significantly with 7 or less on the HAM-D, indicating no depression, 6 a bit of depression, and lower than 6 clearly needing treatment. And, by the way, a score of 10 does not qualify you for bipolar disorder!

These next subsets describe medication challenges with mixed depression and ADHD, and the circumstances of each downturn.

ADHD Medications: Comorbid Depression Missed

If depression is overlooked, and ADHD is treated first with stimulants, the following clinical problems can occur, so watch for them:

Afternoon: Thinking to Depression-Feeling Shift

The initial Stranger Appearance becomes very whiny and fussy in the afternoon after the stimulant wears off. Moods can shift from "I don't care" to, "You hurt my feelings," and becoming inappropriately mad over slight, nonexistent insults. The angry/hurt shift in the afternoon is considered bipolar but often is not, as the depressed moods are revealed after using stimulant meds. This shift is from cognitive/apathy/mental to feelings/hurt/emotional.

Anytime: Thinking to Depression-Feeling Shift

Often the patient is more depressed all day with the stimulant. The shift occurs often sometime in the morning after the stimulant meds are taken. Example: "I've been hurt,

---

32 Hamilton Depression Inventory - the standard test used in depression research

nobody likes me. Now I am hurting more than ever and will just have to stay in my room, forever!" These patients will want to be off the stimulant meds, will do better without stimulants from an emotional/affective point of view, and often do not take stimulant meds on the weekends, diminishing this reaction. Adolescents report that their friends think they are no fun on stimulant medications. Again the shift is from apathy to hurt, but hurt all day. Look for suspect, comorbid depression.

Already Treated For Depression

Some already treated with a stimulant and an antidepressant for comorbid depression become more depressed because they were barely covered by the antidepressant in the first place. Important note: Review the Kelsey Scale above to reconstruct how the antidepressant was working in the first place. If you were running at 5-6 or less, the antidepressant wasn't working. Antidepressant treatment needs to increase or the meds should change. The mood is not likely a result of the stimulant per se, but of the inadequate dose of the antidepressant in the first place.

Clinical Depression Not Identified

The problem with stimulant medications is that they increase dopamine, which has been identified as low with ADHD on measuring brain function in the prefrontal cortex. Increasing dopamine can significantly drop serotonin activity, causing significant depression. The additional dopamine reveals underlying depression not previously seen in the office.

Depression Secondary to ADHD

Stimulants, dopamine, may correct secondary (caused by the ADHD failures) depression, thereby stopping unhappy emotional regressions. Self-dissatisfaction disappears and self-confidence improves. No problem. The depression arose secondary to the failures.

Consider Mood Disorder

If any of these hurt shifts are emotionally dramatic or more severe, consider either mood disorder or these several other possibilities noted below. A good mood history will help predict this downturn. Always remember metabolic issues and drug pathways can create a bipolar appearance.

The Serotonin/Dopamine Seesaw Effect[33]

As you can see, there are several challenges that arise with combining antidepressants with stimulants. And this next one involves neurotransmitter imbalances.[34] *This is the most frequently missed stimulant/serotonin medication interaction.* We are still finding out exactly how this mechanism occurs, but just imagine a seesaw with serotonin on one end and dopamine on the other.

When the serotonin is down, the person is depressed. When the dopamine is down, the person suffers with symptoms of ADHD. An important, often overlooked link exists between dopamine levels and serotonin levels that, if not completely understood, will significantly imbalance most medication outcomes. Treating with only one or the other will drop the

33 http://bit.ly/adhddep
34 Hinz, M, http://www.neuroassist.com More details on serotonin and dopamine imbalance

opposite side of the seesaw. Increasing the neurotransmitters on one side of this seesaw will lower the other side even more if it's already down and that other side isn't simultaneously corrected.

If depression –– decreased serotonin -- is treated first with an antidepressant, comorbid ADHD is aggravated, because serotonin drops the already diminished dopamine.

If ADHD, with that decreased dopamine, is treated first with a stimulant, any depression will become intensified because of this seesaw effect.

Depression often co-exists with ADHD and is frequently missed. With the new guidelines for antidepressant medications, many more individuals are not treated effectively because no specific titration strategies or rules exist for depression either.

ADHD And Anxiety Clinical Appearances

Anxiety, as pointed out earlier, has both cognitive/thinking and affective/feeling components. Remember these observations to enlarge your view of potential treatment interventions.

Cognitive anxiety is often a part of ADHD. In SPECT imaging, several parts of the brain are involved with anxiety. Said another way, all cognitive anxiety is not ADHD, but ADHD is so frequently overlooked as a cognitive anxiety subset it should always be considered as contributory to any anxiety.

Those with only ADHD don't feel as vulnerable as those with comorbid anxiety and depression. Remember that cognitive anxiety, indecision and feeling overwhelmed with an inability to decide, can result in a secondary feeling/affective anxiety.

Agoraphobia Or ADHD With Anxiety?

A woman at an initial medication consult described herself as "depressed for years and uncontrollably anxious." She had recently "freaked out" in a grocery store, and on close questioning, had appeared to be overwhelmed in a claustrophobic way, as if the aisles were closing in. She had been treated for years with anti-anxiety antidepressants and continued to deteriorate, feeling that none of the antidepressants were helping. She felt worse with each new trial of antidepressants and sought a second opinion.

Her anxiety often happened at the grocery store, so often that she and her previous physicians felt that she was also agoraphobic (originally: fear of the marketplace). Both *descriptive diagnoses* were correct, but, functionally, she suffered from two forms of anxiety. She would arrive at the store, become cognitively apprehensive about the shopping experience (recall of previous events), and then become emotionally overwhelmed at *making a wrong choice for her extensive family.*

She simply couldn't decide for everyone, suffered with cognitive anxiety and became overwhelmed with affective anxiety as a result of being unable to shop. She then ran out of the store crying, and "sobbed for hours" in the car. She was tested for ADHD, had a classic school history of ADHD and ultimately responded dramatically with stimulants. Previous attempts to treat her with SSRI antidepressants had aggravated the ADHD, dropped her dopamine and added to her feeling of being overwhelmed, with profound affective consequences. This type of emotionally challenged person is most often considered, by default, bipolar.

She did need an antidepressant with the stimulant, but

low doses of both, watching the seesaw, turned her completely around. The antidepressant alone not only perpetuated the original symptoms, but also contributed to her marked deterioration due to the aggravation of the ADHD by the various multiple serotonin trials.

Understanding this process will very likely result in far fewer people being diagnosed as bipolar, because these specific reactions are so predictable, and once identified, are so easily correctable without heavy mood stabilizers.

Summary: Meds With Depression And ADHD

Remember the seesaw: Stimulant medications for ADHD often make untreated depression worse over time. Watch for the stimulant shifts. These shifts can be corrected with antidepressants. Yes, that means two medications, but "bifocals" often work better because they are more precise for specific issues.

Warning: Drugs for depression often make comorbid ADHD worse over time. Antidepressants, (perhaps many different ones over the years) may leave you with the feeling of being stoned, unable to think or remember, and unable to take antidepressant medication. From a brain imaging perspective, the prefrontal cortex actually "drops out" (shows as hypoperfused measuring regional cerebral blood flow [rCBF] on SPECT imaging) with untreated ADHD and antidepressants. Sometimes bipolar disorder seems likely because this ADHD-based reaction is not immediately identified and appropriately corrected.

Antidepressants with untreated ADHD: Sleeplessness and amplified worries will make one feel quite crazy. Check out the chapter on sleep.

Antidepressants with untreated ADHD: Function and good judgment may diminish over time, while depression at first does appear to improve. Continue to watch for these predictable regressive details if ADHD is associated with depression.

Interaction Warning: Drugs for depression mixed with drugs for ADHD often can have serious interactions. Combining drugs can be tricky and bring a measure of unpredictability. They may work for the short term and then interact months down the road.

Treating ADHD and missing depression: Why depression is missed. Depression is considered only a feeling, an emotional state (sad and blue) and not recognized as a thinking, mental state (I don't care), so it is missed.

The FDA has placed the Black Box warnings on antidepressants. In my opinion, many of these problems with antidepressants occur downstream from unrecognized ADHD. They don't meet criteria for the DSM-4R forms of ADHD, but absolutely meet the criteria for functional ADHD subsets and are repeatedly mistreated from the beginning.

Chapter 8
Furious Minds:
Bipolar And ADHD

Every word or concept, clear as it may seem to be,
has only a limited range of applicability.

Werner Heisenberg, Physicist

Just What Is Bipolar Disorder?

Of all the topics in this book, bipolar disorder often proves to be the most controversial, especially with children who have ADHD. Researchers and clinicians often disagree on the bipolar diagnosis and try to apply adult criteria to the childhood disorder[35]. As Papolos has noted in *The Bipolar Child*,[36] missing the bipolar diagnosis can result in catastrophic regression.

The best psychiatrists argue about multiple aspects of the bipolar diagnosis quite regularly, so the jury is out. There are, according to some authorities, as many as six, and some say seven, different subsets of bipolar, and all depend upon description relative to history. The basic diagnostic manual, the DSM-4R, says there are only three:

Bipolar I - Predominantly Manic with Depression

Bipolar II – Predominantly Depressed with Mania

Cyclothymic - The "soft form" of patterned mood cycles over time

To explain the variations, some use the term "bipolar spectrum" just as some have written about OCD spectrum disorders, to describe the great variety. Genetic studies, brain scans and psychological testing help, but the final common path for deciding about treatment has depended upon mood changes, moods that either appear out of context to the real situation or become too amplified for that situation. Bipolar moods, quite simply, appear too intense, last too long and don't resolve with antidepressants.

With Bipolar: No Absolutes

In the many books written on bipolar disorder, one common theme emerges: Bipolar is a mood disorder, often

35 Goodwin, F, *The Infinite Mind*: http://www.lcmedia.com/mind133.htm

36 Papolos, D, and Papolos, J, *The Bipolar Child*, Broadway, 2002.

with exaggerated ups and downs, some psychotic and some not psychotic. Smaller ups and downs don't provide enough specific symptoms for researchers to measure. Soon after that simple observation, diagnostic matters often fall into disarray with often heated dispute. The professional arguments look, at times, like overt manifestations of bipolar disorder.

Even though many in academia challenge the suggestion of ADHD occurring in association with bipolar disorder, many practitioners disagree. Those of us in the trenches have managed these two disorders simultaneously for many years with the same patients over thousands of hours. Our evidence contradicts that of researchers. Just ask any informed clinical psychopharmacologist who regularly works in an office setting.

The researchers are, however, quite correct in documenting the serious and often life-threatening problems that can occur with only half the diagnosis. Depression, ADHD and any other specific biologic disorders occurring with bipolar disorder each need their own specific system of intervention.

Bipolar And ADHD: What To Do

Bipolar disorder is frequently confused with ADHD and associated with ADHD. Since the debate springs up so often, it remains quite surprising that so many researchers have concluded that ADHD should not be treated if found with bipolar disorder. Some even say ADHD simply doesn't exist with bipolar, that the bipolar disorder is causing the cognitive challenges. The trench providers uniformly disagree with the tenured researchers.

Often those who discuss bipolar illness take the either/or view: Is it either bipolar or ADHD? This reminds me of the parallel problem with addictions. Did you know that, according to many, drug addicts and alcoholics suffer only from addiction and have no "dual diagnosis?" Or if they do, certainly it can't be ADHD, or that ADHD treatment would interfere with the "treatment!"

In my practice we find very few patients with either/or, and many with yes/and: both bipolar and ADHD. So just what does that bipolar spectrum look like?

Bipolar Symptoms:

Rages lasting far longer than expected, from one-and-a-half up to seven hours

Long periods of sleep deprivation; days to weeks

Manic behavior, feelings of omnipotence, that they can, for example, fly

Hypersexual, and crossing sexual boundaries without thinking of consequences

Racing thoughts, pressure of speech, irrational demands for special treatment

Depression and rages aggravated by antidepressants

Rages and depression aggravated by stimulants

Uncontrollable, irrational substance abuse

Family history of mood disorder

None of these are diagnostic, but any of these symptoms should raise the concern for careful medical intervention as outlined in this chapter.

Walks Like Bipolar, Talks Like Bipolar, But Is It?

Below is a partial list of biologic challenges that look like bipolar disorder. They may meet requirements for bipolar from the surface, but may prove correctable without mood stabilizers, and may ultimately prove not to be primarily bipolar.

Psychiatric drug-to-drug interactions

Drug interactions with medications from other medical
providers

Medication reactions based upon CYP 450 genetics, 2D6
for example

Drug reactions based upon incorrect diagnosis in the first
place, such as more than depression

Sleep problems

Brain injury, post-concussive syndrome

Lyme Disease[37]

Psychomotor epilepsy

Malnutrition with specific, measurable, neurotransmitter
deficiencies; picky eaters, anorexia, bulimarexia

Vegetarian, not corrected for nutritional insufficiencies

Hormone dysregulations: Estrogen dominance,
adrenal fatigue

Stress

Post-Traumatic Stress Disorder

Immune dysfunction: wheat (gluten) sensitivity,
milk (casein) sensitivity

Polycystic ovarian syndrome, PMS, PMDD, Postpartum
Depression, Estrogen Dominance

Adrenal and pituitary disorders

Thyroid disorders

Chronic disease: Crohn's, IBS, constipation, leaky gut, GERD

---

37 Notes on a significant new test to determine Lyme disease: MyLyme ID.

Chronic use of over-the-counter medications

Inflammatory conditions with consequent brain dysregulation

Dementia/inflammation secondary to environmental toxins

Drug, alcohol and other addictions

Combinations of several of these

ADHD with emotional dysregulation[38]

Identifying these complex challenges will take your medical team much further down the road than simply augmenting with another mood stabilizer. As I have pointed out so regularly here, we may have some impact on the symptoms, but without specific targets, we will, over time, remain lost. And, furthermore, many of these same disturbances appear clinically as ADHD.

One common, reassuring thread to all of these challenging conditions is that they all have measurable metabolic fingerprints that will help with those next steps. More evidence will suggest additional strategies.

Treating Bipolar And ADHD Simultaneously

The Golden Rules for using medications in complex presentations are: Pay attention to the multiple objectives with each diagnosis, watch the reactions carefully for the therapeutic window therapeutic with each medication and most importantly, move even more slowly, using lower doses than recommended.

Address the mood disorder first: Yes, I am repeating myself, but it does bear repeating. If stimulants and antidepressants can dysregulate the bipolar brain, start by correcting the cracks in the bipolar foundation first. Follow

38 Barkley, R, *ADHD in Adults: What the Science Says* 2007

the most predictable intervention system for the best results. Address ADHD only in sequence, after significant moods are successfully managed. Think emotions first, cognition last.

Mind racing does not make the diagnosis of bipolar: Chronic "unmanageable cognitive abundance" is not synonymous with bipolar disorder. Many suffer with profound cognitive worry, few affective problems and only occasional impulsivity. "Mind racing" can present in the context of a simple, uncomplicated, ADHD diagnosis.

With symptoms of bipolar always prioritize sleep: During any medical intervention for complex multiple diagnoses, sleep must be addressed. Sleep deprivation frequently results in marked emotional and cognitive deterioration. ADHD and bipolar disorder can both significantly dysregulate sleep and contribute to cognitive ADHD symptoms. Carefully assess all sleep patterns from the outset, and treat sleep carefully at the same time as treating ADHD.

Multiple meds require more informed awareness of drug interactions: These have been previously reviewed.

Rule out brain injury and metabolic issues: Numerous metabolic and neurotransmitter biomarker assessments can prove exceedingly helpful in reviewing the underlying causes of the mood disorder, and are often clinically indicated upon careful medical review. Brain imaging is a useful tool for assessing mild or severe traumatic brain injury. Metabolic illness and traumatic brain injury can both contribute to bipolar disorder symptoms.

Summary: Treating Bipolar With ADHD

Start with the angry moods first, depression next, then stimulant medications. Stay focused on treating the moods regardless of the disputed diagnosis.

ADHD does come in many forms, and one is irritation and anger. New non-stimulant medications, such as Intuniv, may have a positive impact on mood dysregulation secondary to ADHD.

Molecular, cellular and metabolic testing for specific neurophysiologic imbalances will be the standard of care in the future, and are easily available.

Even lower cost, less complicated neurotransmitter testing, supported by many insurance programs, can prove helpful in offering specific alternatives for many of these challenging treatment and diagnostic presentations.

"Ring of Fire" (Amen's term, often proffered as synonymous with bipolar presentations) is a brain appearance, a SPECT finding, not a diagnosis, and does not correlate with bipolar illness unless other symptoms present clinically. The correct term, used by other nuclear medicine physicians, is "diffuse cortical hyperperfusion," and indicates a significant hypermetabolic state . Its metabolic origin is unclear and needs more careful review. Hypermetabolism is just that, a functional brain process, not a DSM-4R diagnosis.

SPECT findings do not correlate with DSM-4R diagnosis because, for one reason, SPECT is a functional and DSM-4R is only descriptive.

Dr. Papolos[39] points out that *ninety-four percent* of bipolar kids will meet the criteria for ADHD, suggesting that informed and careful intervention is essential. Working from the perspective of only one diagnosis in these complicated cases often proves counterproductive.

Differentiate bipolar from both traumatic brain injury and from ADHD.

---

39 Papolos, D, and Papolos, J, *The Bipolar Child*, Broadway, 2002.

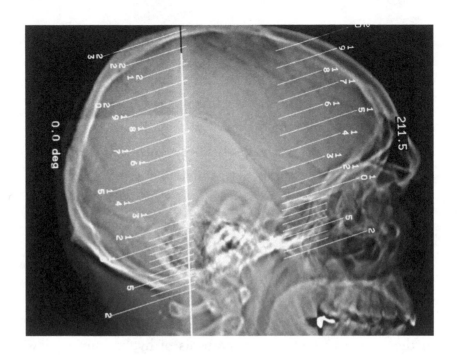

Chapter 9
Unpredictable:
Brain Injury And ADHD

A man should look for what is,
and not for what he thinks should be.

Albert Einstein

Brain Injury And ADHD: Gasoline On The Fire

Brain injuries exaggerate pre-existing ADHD. Those with
Traumatic Brain Injury (TBI) combined with ADHD often
remain untreatable unless correctly diagnosed right at the

outset. Many lifetimes are wasted with confusing symptoms, moods and treacherously impulsive behaviors.

TBI is the great mind-mystery diagnosis with many disguises. Thinking and feeling imbalances abound, and TBI remains remarkably unresponsive to traditional medications. Many of the best practitioners don't recognize TBI and simply don't ask about it in the patient's history. Even if the patient has been diagnosed with TBI, neurologists often treat brain-traumatized individuals as epileptics, and psychiatrists often use familiar medications to treat TBI as bipolar disorder.

After having seen thousands of SPECT brain scans, I can report with utmost certainty that TBI is often overlooked and is more frequently found in SPECT. Brain injury often appears in the scans as asymmetrical patterns of hypoperfusion, low blood flow, diminished metabolism. Frequently patients do not remember the injury until they actually see images of their brain during the office evaluation, the actual SPECT review process. Injuries from years ago remain easily visible with SPECT and can remain actively problematic throughout a lifetime.

Both Patients And Caregivers Suffer

Caring medical practitioners often miss TBI with associated ADHD, miss the associated depression, miss the issues I've discussed here with drug interactions, and resort to high doses of whatever meds will control the moods. The result: weight gain, depression, deterioration and substance abuse. TBI creates many long-term medical and psychiatric issues for both patients and caregivers. TBI treatment has not kept up with rapidly advancing brain science.

Providers And Family In Denial – The Patient Knows

Recently I saw a middle-aged man after he'd had an undeniable brain injury, a concussion causing significant emotional changes and an increasing problem managing his business because of large cognitive blank spots in ordinary conversation. His family had denied his previously diagnosed ADHD, and the brain injury continued untreated because all medical practitioners said they had no further treatments. His professional life, emotional life and cognitive life in a shambles, he increased drinking and smoking pot.

Neither his family nor physicians understood the ADHD problem and remained clueless about treatment options. But they did know he was drinking -- an uncanny grasp of the obvious.

He was sent to a nationally recognized substance abuse treatment program for the drinking problem. The easiest diagnosis gets the attention. Quite typically, as is often seen in addiction treatment, the "recovery center" itself remains in profound denial of many deeper contributory variables with substance abuse. The center had no treatment strategies, in fact had negative reactions to his treatment plan for ADHD. They had only a passing interest with no workup for recovering TBI, and couldn't understand why he left the program prematurely.

Does overwhelming, untreated boredom and ADHD sound like an unreasonable reaction in the context of his multiple cognitive problems? Would you stay if you suffered with cognitive problems that interfered with your focus and concentration, and everyone kept missing two (ADHD and TBI) undeniable pre-existing core problems while compulsively repeating the sobriety mantra?

Does the blind leading the blind come to mind? Who takes responsibility for confronting denial?

I am working with this patient on a variety of metabolic issues, including neurotransmitter balance, gut issues and significant metabolic challenges that could hamper brain and body healing. He remains sober and on stimulant medication, improving and rethinking his life.

Problems For The Medical Team

To complicate already confusing symptomatic matters, TBI patients are often difficult to manage. They communicate poorly. They remain confused about directions. They rationalize noncompliance. Their fury often remains completely unvarnished and they often cross social boundaries with impunity.

The most challenging hurdle for practitioners is mastering the complicated molecular and cellular physiology of brain function as it relates to psychiatric conditions. Laboratory testing alone is inconclusive. Brain science is daunting; it's actually much more complex than understanding how to use SPECT scans for treatment evidence in the office.

The Molecular Evolution Is Already Here

We all have some more work to do.

I am grateful for having learned SPECT imaging, and still use it regularly in my practice. As you can see from my comments, SPECT brain imaging applies well for diagnosing and initially recognizing the pathology of TBI. But now it's time to take those earlier SPECT lessons to the next plateau, from macro SPECT diagnosis to the micro diagnostic laboratory. Practitioners should design specific treatment plans for the neurons themselves. Mind treatment evolves through precision in measurement. Diagnosis provides targeted content; treatment needs to focus on more specific biologic processes –- the dynamics of neurophysiologic recovery vs. simply medications for control.

Neuroscience evidence changes thinking in the way clinicians measure thinking activities, and the process of thinking for the patient. Neuroscience changes your questions.

Precise neuroscience evidence dramatically changes health delivery and health applications on many levels. Precise molecular and cellular diagnoses dramatically improve specific recovery protocols and prognosis for the toughest psychiatric treatment conditions -- from ADHD, to depression, to bipolar, to brain injury, to addictions[40] -- improve dramatically.

SPECT is helpful, but clearly only gives superficial, less than adequate directions *for the treatment process itself.* SPECT does improve on contemporary office diagnostics, but falls short in the translation-to-application process.

Some SPECT centers have simply taken the helpful SPECT findings and developed some protocols for psychiatric treatment. But routine SPECT findings subsequently associated with routine recommendations perpetuate the homogenization and the commoditization of mental health. They miss the reality of the individual patient, the reality of the more complex, specific set of molecular and cellular processes that are inevitably dysregulated.

---

40 Addiction medicine and the recovery process also improves - http://bit.ly/dpre-covery

I've repeatedly seen SPECT diffuse cortical hyperperfusion, "Ring of Fire," associated with specific measurable metabolic imbalances, most frequently immune dysregulation caused by a great variety of antigens. That "Ring of Fire" resulted in a "bipolar" diagnosis that was encouraged by both the scan pictures and within the moods discussed during the office history. The most persuasive findings arrived with the precise laboratory results. Greater accuracy equals greater predictability with treatment. The answers to the laboratory questions are far beyond the scope of this book, but for multiple webinars and testing recommendations see the links to the laboratories at the end of this book.

Two simple examples: treating milk allergies significantly corrected a psychotic bipolar presentation. Copper intoxication measured through hair analysis and subsequently corrected extinguished visual and auditory hallucinations with suicidal ideation in a young girl headed for college.

Bottom Line On Brain Measurements

SPECT helps to diagnose TBI. But new laboratory measurements can improve neurophysiologically-based treatment strategies and cost much less. Both have a specific focus and improve upon the old process of making diagnosis by appearances and history. Laboratory tests evaluate cellular and molecular function. If cost is an issue, skip SPECT and go for the testing.

Medications: TBI And ADHD

Those with TBI are very sensitive to medical intervention, specifically stimulant meds, and any others for comorbid conditions, such as antidepressants for depression.

If TBI is overlooked, the stimulant meds and any variety of new meds simply don't work effectively, and they often make the patient worse. And ADHD medications used for those with brain injury must be titrated, as previously indicated, much more carefully than for patients with no TBI.

This different, more careful, attitude with TBI medication objectives can significantly improve treatment outcomes. TBI often demonstrates associated ADHD problems, and after the impulsivity and anger from the injury has been treated, one can carefully set about treating the ADHD –- with all of the care suggested in the previous chapter on bipolar disorder.

Ask Yourself About Brain Injury

Clinical evidence and the scientific literature contain numerous references to ADHD symptoms occurring simultaneously with brain injury. Often brain injury will aggravate a pre-existing ADHD. Multiple injuries can draw down the brain reserve, its ability to compensate and regenerate from injury.

Brain injury and brain damage can significantly improve with a number of new intervention systems that fall out of the "FDA approved" category into the anecdotal-experience-does-count category. One option is neuroplasticity (the brain regenerating itself under improved growing conditions). Neurofeedback, retraining, nutraceuticals, exercise and improved diet can all help. And they can be undertaken simultaneously. Research protocols deal with outdated DSM-4R diagnostic profiles, compromising the intervention opportunities. Continue to watch for protocols that document progress with both pharmaceutical and non-pharmaceutical interventions.

Simultaneous, informed applications of both pharmaceutical and non-pharmaceutical interventions for TBI and associated ADHD offer considerable hope. The challenge is in knowing the interactions and expectations with both intervention systems for a more comprehensive response, as some neurotransmitters create their own imbalances. Monotherapy, using only one medication, is outdated and contradicted by modern medical research.

Consider Your Brain Reserve

Prepare yourself for the journey. You, as a patient, will have to take on more responsibility, which means taking better care of yourself. It will not be easy. Don't rely on professionals who haven't kept up with the evolving field of core brain findings. Seeking the most modern and informed doctors is the patient's responsibility. Brain literature and science is growing so fast that even those interested in brain physiology have trouble keeping up. I have decided in these pages to run with the applications most commonly proven by positive responses in the literature and the laboratory. This guide is in an effort to make your next steps less complicated, but it will be outdated soon simply because of the dramatic improvements in laboratory technology. Stay tuned for new developments.

Healing The Brain Reserve

Some of you will have to change your diet and stick with that change if it's indicated. Some will have to take multiple vitamin/cofactor supplements to re-grow brain cells, or other supplements to help with your chronic, metabolic, under-the-radar illness. Recovery will be harder at first and most often becomes easier, with less challenging variables and strategies over time. It will be easier when you begin to see improvement.

Supporting your brain reserve, your internal nutritional metabolic pool of healing resources, will take time. Your brain reserve is not just a simple place found in your brain. It's almost impossible to measure without using highly specific laboratory assessment tools, repeated over time. Your brain reserve is cellular and molecular.

Brain injury is now, belatedly, a hot topic with the National Football League. TBI can now be recognized by SPECT functional brain imaging. Your brain reserve is used up more quickly with every additional injury. And, in case you didn't realize it, your brain takes much longer to heal than your tongue, for example. Burned tongue cells regenerate every 3 days. Brain cells take months or years to recover. Neuroplasticity -- brain growth -- is a hot neuroscience topic that shows great promise for speeding up recovery.

Determination to succeed, and a treatment program that goes beyond simply diagnosis into highly specific intervention processes, can turn the recovery tide.

First, Ask Yourself Specifics About Brain Injury

Some of the key questions:

1. Did you have an injury, hard hit to the head and see stars even without losing consciousness? Even whiplash can cause brain injury.

2. Do you suffer frequent severe, terrifying dreams and fears of sleeping that result in insomnia? Severe night symptoms can be associated with TBI. Nightmares, impulsivity and paranoid

thinking may be more than biologically based, as differentiated from the psychological borderline personality.

3. Do you feel, upon going to sleep, that a primal darkness is coming over you, or do you have feelings that others are in the room when they aren't?

4. Are you forgetful, more than others, and may have had toxic exposure from activities like working in a paint shop, chemistry lab, dying T- shirts? All of these can cause a toxic brain injury. Think "poisoned neurons."

5. Do you lose your temper and terrify others while you are thinking you are simply expressing yourself?

6. Do you have anger that comes and goes, one that is easy for you, very hard for others, and no remorse about it?

7. Is your sleep dysregulated since that injury, with severe insomnia and heavy napping during the day?

8. Do you feel exhaustion all the time, just can't get out of bed and can't think clearly when you do (adrenal fatigue secondary to the shock and stress, post TBI)?

9. Do you have vague neurologic symptoms with dizziness, headache and imbalance, or confusion that comes and goes?

These questions don't begin to cover every symptom, but do suggest further inquiry. See this TBI checklist[41] to assess yourself more completely.

Previous Brain Injury Studies Were Negative

Often MRI, CAT, CT anatomic and static scans used to review possible brain damage may have been negative in your past. You were relieved to have had no problems. If you do have problems suggestive of TBI, this would be time to consider more

41 Brain injury checklist: http://dpi.wi.gov/sped/pdf/tbi-checklist.pdf

functional, less static review with studies such as SPECT, PET or fMRI.

With Dramatic Atypical Responses to Stimulants

Any dramatically regressive changes with stimulant medications suggest underlying metabolic and structural/ neurologically based brain problems that need further investigation. Stimulants for ADHD may prove to be the canary in the coal mine with an odd, paradoxical, over-stimulated reaction on low doses. Look for associated issues such as toxicity, brain injury, immune dysfunction, depression, and bipolar illness, even constipation. Actually constipation, of all the metabolic challenges, is the most frequent explanation for atypical reactions to stimulant medications.

If TBI is missed, the stimulant meds will cause profound unpredictable reactions. Misdiagnosis often follows with mounting hours and costs for care.

Brain Injury, Not Bipolar

Start with these overview perspectives:

ADHD often will show remorse for anger; bipolar shows only a little remorse. TBI shows almost no remorse, doesn't even see the anger, or blames it on circumstance. Anger denial, from actual content to intensity in the process, abounds with TBI.

Bipolar anger lasts for hours. TBI lasts shorter periods of time, and extinguishes quickly.

TBI intensity looks angrier, more intense, and is less related to the real circumstances. Blame abounds.

Bipolar often shows more narcissism: "I am cool, you are

stupid." TBI often isn't concerned with being cool or anyone's perceptions at all.

ADHD symptoms are more cognitive, with thinking worries that have escalated. Bipolar is more affective, justified in being angry at the inappropriate world. TBI is worrying, thinking, more paranoid, and often even more sleep deprived and even less appropriate inhibition in expression. Drug and alcohol intoxication look like TBI, completely irrational and toxic. Substance abusers are suffering from brain damage on a cellular level. The obvious point is that substance abuse with either bipolar or TBI requires sobriety for the long haul to recover.

Sleep problems with TBI don't occur in cycles. They appear, almost always, as a continuous problem. Bipolar sleep patterns cycle. ADHD patterns usually involve Level 1 and 2 sleep, and often arise under long periods of cognitive, overwhelming stress and then cause the insomnia to last an entire night.

TBI and bipolar don't need stress to keep them up; they are storming anyway. ADHD sleep disorders are contextual, stress related.

Testing is necessary for the most challenging presentations for all of these conditions from ADHD, including bipolar, TBI and substance abuse. With poor response, or plateau response, one needs, at the very least, a complete metabolic assessment of oxidative stress, amino acids, neurotransmitters medication mixes, nutritional status and immune dysregulations. If you don't know how your body is working in the first place, how can medications have any predictability? It sounds complicated, but several labs are available that will provide deeper understanding for more specific interventions.

ADHD will have some respect for caretakers, bipolar

has less, TBI almost none, and substance abuse sends mixed messages to potential caretakers.

Summary: Treating TBI With ADHD

If it looks like a possible TBI challenge, ask your medical team to consider injury and go only with small doses of stimulant medication.

Adjust those small doses very slowly, watching carefully for the top of the Therapeutic Window.

Differentiate bipolar from TBI.

Lithium is not the standard of care with TBI.

You can use stimulant medications for the ADHD after the brain becomes stabilized.

Look for a practitioner who understands the neurotransmitter issues and molecular and cellular physiology of brain activity, as well as the measurement process. These folks may be difficult to find now, but in the near future they will set the standard for care.

With diagnosed TBI you should find someone skilled with neurotransmitter, amino acid, oxidative stress testing.

TBI includes all the brain injury, toxic exposures and sleep apnea.

Treat your sleep apnea on every level, from exercise to metabolic correction.

Consider other interventions for TBI such as Hyperbaric Oxygen Treatment (HBOT)[42]. Even small increases of atmospheric pressure can significantly improve brain function, even though your insurance company may not pay for it.

---

42 Hyperbaric Oxygen Wikipedia: http://en.wikipedia.org/wiki/HBOT

Consider other intervention processes such as neurofeedback, interactive metronome[43] and various neurophysiologic enhancement activities.

Plan to get regular exercise. Brain cells don't recover well with reduced oxygen.

---

43 Interactive metronome: http://www.interactivemetronome.com/IMPublic/Home. aspx

Chapter 10
Shoot For Your Therapeutic Window

It doesn't matter how beautiful your theory is,
it doesn't matter how smart you are.
If it doesn't agree with experiment, it's wrong.

Richard P. Feynman, Physicist

Now that the ADHD targets and their imitators are fleshed, let's figure out how those medications actually work over time. The operational concept for the rest of *New ADHD Medication Rules*: first know your target, then know the expected actions, the trajectories of each medication, and finally know how to specifically measure brain and body variables when you don't hit the target.

The good news is that you can fix the body and brain variables that create problems after you first know what the outcomes should be. When you know what you are shooting at, and what you are shooting, the other things that change the outcomes can then be measured and corrected. Yes, many should measure the body and brain variables before they start in the first place.

You may remember the importance of that old standard of using body weight measurements to predict medication outcomes. Some of the stimulants do cause appetite challenges. But with the new information on genetics and metabolic pathways, we now know that weight is but one small factor in adjusting the dosage correctly. The most important new caveat: think metabolically; think functionally regarding brain and body interactions. These next chapters will tell you in easy steps just how to do that.

The metabolic burn rate helps pinpoint the best dosage and medication combinations. Proper dosage with stimulant medications provides the best outcomes, with the least side effects and the most predictability from the outset. Predictability is one of my favorite concepts; I hope it becomes one of yours.

What You Don't Know *Can* Hurt You

If you don't read this next section, you will simply not understand the specifics of what your medical team is trying to accomplish. The Therapeutic Window will teach you about potential problems, will guide you on the process of what to consider next, and will tell you what to report to your medical team over time. The Therapeutic Window process must become your new best friend.

Having written many thousands of new stimulant medication prescriptions, I can tell you with considerable certainty that we often don't get dosages right on the first visit, even if we know what to expect.

Therapeutic Window adjustments are not medication experimentation on office "lab rats or guinea pigs," as some assume, but simply creating customized treatment. Think of brain optometry. If you wear glasses or contacts, you know very well that you had to sit in a chair while the optometrist repeatedly went over the question: "Which can you see best, this or this?"

Cookie-cutter glasses just don't work over time, even though the prescription might be correct on the first visit. The reason for therapeutic trials is that we must measure the burn rate variables by using the medication with the person. Burn rates vary and biologic impediments vary -- so let's start by fully understanding the basic measurements. Furthermore, that's why we measure burn rate specifics on every medication check.

The Therapeutic Window Spelled Out

We should all be more careful with these stimulant medications and titrate (adjusting the dose). If we adjust dosages according to reported research, we often will not get the dose right. Research is for safety and efficacy with large numbers, for FDA approval. Often it does not encapsulate multiple challenges discovered while working with your own medical team.

Use the process of finding your personal Therapeutic Window as exploration with your own mind map. The Therapeutic Window shows the place, the exact dosage, where the stimulant medication used for ADHD works best. If medication dosage is outside of the window, it simply is not working correctly, triggering a range of frustration and disappointment.

After recognizing these fundamental Window lessons, you will become an essential partner in the complicated process of medication dosage adjustment. Without this essential information, medication adjustment becomes a roll of the dice, and reactions will occur frequently because, "How do you feel?" is but a small and inaccurate measure of subtle processes of each person's metabolic activity. Individualized treatment is disregarded. Commoditization[44] and homogenization[45] lead to treatment failures.

There are three main points to assess in your window, and each will have specific characteristics for you that are often quite different than those experienced by others who take the same medication: The Top, The Sides and The Bottom. If medications are correctly adjusted, you will live right inside that Therapeutic Window with no side effects and a good response. You won't go out the top, nor will you bump on the bottom, you'll float right inside.

The Top Of The Therapeutic Window:
7 Tips For The Top

The first objective is no side effects. If the medication is just right in dosage and duration you will feel a good effect, and that you are simply floating through that effective Window opening, no problem, and no, or very few, side effects.

----

44 Commoditization: When price alone determines the difference in process
45 Homogenization: When multiple variables are excluded encouraging no variation in properties

Top: Clinical Example

An executive with whom I have been adjusting dosage is so pleased with his new ability to concentrate that he is seeking to get more out of his day. In spite of the fact that I am carefully asking him about Duration of Effectiveness (DOE), he asserts that it "just isn't working as well as it should." He says his DOE in Vyvanse is from 7 a.m. to 5 p.m. for a ten-hour DOE, so I increase him from 40 mg to 50 mg in the morning, knowing that he will likely extend his DOE up to about two more hours in the evening. Increasing Vyvanse 10 mg in the morning adds about two hours to the afternoon DOE.

He returns on the next medication check saying that it just isn't working in the morning the way it did previously, and he needs more. On careful questioning he reported that it "hits well about 10 a.m., lasts until about 2 p.m., drops out and then kicks in again in the evening. The evening is covered, but now the morning is a problem." On further questioning, he had new challenges with insomnia, appetite diminished with weight loss and a feeling of anxious pressure through the day. He felt that more medication would solve the increase in worries and resolve the morning challenge.

Actually this report typifies a subtle key sign of coming out the Top, so I dropped him back to 30 mg, worked back to 40 mg, and he discovered that he was doing much better both in the morning and afternoon. His burn rate, his DOE, was eleven hours, quite acceptable for Vyvanse. He no longer was bouncing out the top.

The Seven Top Tips

1. If the medication is too much, too high in dosage, you will have signs of toxicity, and will hit the top, bump your head on the top of that window. At the top you become more irritable, sometimes depressed, unfocused or hyperfocused, lose your appetite, have difficulty sleeping well, or feel stoned. Consider lowering the dose. It's often not the medication, but the dosage.

2. All-Day Problems: Toxicity may appear as absolute: All-day buzzing and can't think, just out the top of the window, feeling stoned or so full of thoughts you can't get anything done. This requires a lower dosage.

3. On and Off All-Day Problems: Toxicity may appear as cyclical, mercurial -- off and on -- with hyperfocus and subsequent inability to focus. This is the most frequently missed side effect at the top, and the most important clinically, because it encourages regular, predictable negative med consequences. Most often with amphetamine products such as Adderall IR, Adderall XR, Vyvanse and Dexedrine, a person out the Top of the Window will have periods of hyperfocus appearing later in the morning (took it at 7 a.m. and it didn't work until 10 a.m.), then fluctuations later in the day. It looks like the meds are almost working, and is often confused with the bottom of the window: not enough. Adjusting dosage upward, without recognizing this essential Top of the Window problem can become toxic and out of control.

4. "Feeling Drugged" Is Too Much: Simply feels like you are toxic; it's just too much. You shouldn't feel stoned or drugged;

your mind should work better, not worse.

5. More Symptoms at the Top: Confusion, disorientation, forgetfulness intensifies, cognitive stress, anxiety each increased, while self-expression diminishes. You just can't think as well.

6. Different Stimulant, Different Tops: Stimulants adjusted incorrectly leave you feeling moody and depressed all day, and relieved in the evening as they have a shorter half-life with an expected duration of less than fourteen. If you feel better when they are gone from your system, this is a big hint. With amphetamine stimulants too high you might feel buzzed, intense, overly attentive, angry and sad mood swings. Switching to methylphenidate ("Ritalin-like") products you may feel more "stoned and out of it" if meds are adjusted above the Top of the Window.

7. Start low: If the duration is longer than expected for that specific medication, you are simply too high, figuratively and literally. If you feel these kind of symptoms for the first couple of days after starting a new med, there's usually no problem. If symptoms continue, an adjustment is very likely necessary. Never start using an expected dose (always use less than expected), and never plan to adjust upward without thinking about this window.

The Bottom of The Therapeutic Window:
7 Tips for the Bottom

It's puzzling how often folks, who come into the office for a second opinion, don't have a clear idea of when the medication isn't working. It does make complete sense that if they don't know what they are shooting at they won't know if they hit it.

Bottom: Clinical Example

A male patient, electrical engineer, age 45, with a history of significant constipation (bowel movement only once or twice a week) his whole life and a history of severe head injury with concussion who has ADHD: both head injury and constipation predict a specific sensitivity to stimulant medication, and that he will likely metabolize stimulant meds more slowly.

After starting with a very low dose of medication, it was clear that his DOE was much shorter than expected. The medication only lasted until noon when he had taken it at 5:30 in the morning. Because of his various metabolic challenges I increased his meds slowly to find the right dose to keep him off the Bottom.

The Seven Bottom Tips

1. Again start with the DOE. If you feel no effect, and any of the objective treatment target measures from the first visit are not corrected, or if they were corrected for only two to three days and lost, then the bottom has not been adequately reached.

2. Energy and weight loss are inappropriate targets for the bottom. Train even the youngest members of your family to understand what the treatment is about so they can participate in discussing effective action. Often children are not consulted, so you and your team need to establish exactly what you expect. Remember, the newest drugs are cleaner and provide more clearly cognitive results, not as many energy and endurance

results. Energy and endurance are metabolic issues, not ADHD issues, and while stimulants may work for those problems they will ultimately prove ineffective and often require megadosing for underlying adrenal or metabolic issues. Stimulants do not correct hormonal, adrenal, thyroid or malnutrition problems, though they may appear corrective on the front end of treatment.

3. If you are taking IR Immediate Release Adderall, for example, it should last five to six hours, not three to four. If it only lasts three to four hours, it should be increased to reach the expected DOE.

4. Cover the entire day. Long ago we recognized that school and work serve as important treatment objectives and need specific focus, but agreed that family life is just as important. Adjust the medication dosages, even the IR doses, so they last into the evening. Family matters -– in spite of what some in managed care think. None of the IR (Immediate Release) short acting doses last past noon without significant side effects. With managed care so supportive of IR medications working only from the cost perspective, many have suggested increasing the morning IR stimulant doses so that they last into the afternoon, hoping to get through school. Bad idea. Too much medication can become toxic in the morning and inadequate for the afternoon.

5. Look for specifics with the bottom and the afternoon drop. With Vyvanse the bottom is murkier and more associated with a thinking correction than somatic/feeling response. With Adderall, either XR or IR, the afternoon drop is often more

precipitous and obvious. It's important to be precise on the DOE expectation of each specific medication. If Vyvanse only lasts eight hours, it is underdosed. If Ritalin IR lasts only three hours, it is underdosed. Daytrana is tricky because it can last, but the dose may be insufficiently effective during the day. Best to measure Daytrana effectiveness with the effective Post Patch Time (PPT). It should still be working about three hours after the patch is removed.

6. Don't let worries about addiction keep you from correcting the Bottom. You will not have medical withdrawal problems on FDA-approved dosages, even with slightly more than FDA-approved dosages, if used as I am indicating here. The only problems I have had with any of my patients are those that develop their own treatment/abuse plan, without informing me.

7. If you feel a medication isn't working consider that it simply may be too high a dosage. Remember, the Bottom and the Top can feel the same.

The Sides Of The Therapeutic Window: Seven Tips for the Sides

Looking for the sides of the Therapeutic Window is easy. If you understand how to use the sides as guideposts over time, it will actually be difficult to create a significant problem with adjusting your medications. It's so easy that my entire medical staff uses it with every medication check, and everyone I have mentored has used it for years routinely, with no difficulties.

Knowing and using the side measures will help you and your team with medication predictability, precision and efficacy.

Take the measurement in the morning and then when the meds stop working. DOE is the measured time between.

The Sides will help you with all of the metabolic questions, with adjustment over time if a child is growing up, even for adjustments with other medications that have short DOEs. Just dial the medication in with your medical team, and once you learn how to give the feedback, it is very difficult to make mistakes. Further, this tool can be used as long as you take stimulant medications. It doesn't matter if you go to Hong Kong and have to switch medications because that med isn't available. You can adjust using *Rules*.

Sides: Clinical Example

A patient starts on 30 mg of Vyvanse taken at 7 a.m. and it is out at noon, about a five-hour DOE. Expectation for Vyvanse DOE is twelve-to-fourteen hours. Common sense would indicate we could jump up considerably to 60 mg, if you wanted to guess the next dose and projected time expectation. Stimulant medications simply don't work in that kind of predictable way. In fact they are rather idiosyncratic.

I always take it slower on this next increase. I ask patients to wait about two weeks, taking their time to unmistakably recognize when they reach at the other side of the window. That next adjustment should be dialed in at nearly perfect.

The Seven Side Tips
The Sides Of The Window Are Based Upon Time:

1. The Expected DOE of that specific medication for that specific person's metabolic rate must be customized from the outset and throughout the duration of treatment. Every person

burns medications at different rates that cannot be predicted by superficial appearances of weight or size. I have an ex-Navy commander who stands about six-foot-six and has to duck when he comes in the door. He takes only Adderall 10 mg XR and the DOE is a reasonable ten hours. We want to have a specific match between expected duration and clinically effective duration.

2. Know The Medication DOE Expectations From The Outset: Some studies disagree with some of the next points on specific medications I am about to discuss. Pharmaceutical companies have done their homework and are focused on these same DOE objectives. I simply disagree with some of their DOE findings. My own studies involve thousands of patient hours over years of treatment using a determined, every-visit focus on this Window grid.

3. Start Working: Measure precisely the DOE for every medication check. Ask "When did you take it and when does it stop working?" If taken at seven in the morning and it lasts until three in the afternoon, that is the DOE. **The math is simple:** five hours in the morning plus three in the afternoon. A medication might work for eight hours, but still blow the person out the Top of the Window if it's an IR and pushed too high, beyond the expected DOE of six hours.

4. The First Side Objective, Morning Onset: All meds should be working in thirty-to-forty-five minutes. IR (Immediate Release) tablets have a fast onset, but the sides of the IR window are too narrow, lasting only a short part of the day. IR meds need to be taken two-to-three times daily because the DOE is

far too short. If the **morning onset** is more than forty-five minutes, the dose isn't right.

5. Breakfast is Essential: Protein breakfast works best and most often. With meds, since we are now paying attention to the rate of metabolism, the DOE, we are much more interested in "rate limiting steps." Breakfast prevents irritation of the gastric mucosa (stomach lining). With breakfast, that early onset side of the morning "Window" is gentler with fewer uncomfortable peaks.

6. When Time Release Stops Working: The extended-release capsules from Concerta to Adderall XR are all mechanically released and have unpredictable release times based upon acid/base variables in the stomach and bowel, and upon the transit time of the bowel contents. Long transit time often means greater sensitivity to meds and a relative accumulation of meds over time, narrowing of the Window. Metabolic challenges with bowel function almost always change the afternoon release time when the meds stop working. Vyvanse is not as vulnerable to rate changes based upon acid/base balance or transit time, as the prodrug release is from enzymes in the red blood cells.

7. Afternoon Release with Vyvanse: Vyvanse deserves its own tip because it is so effective, with such an excellent, predictable twelve-to-fourteen hour DOE. The metabolically released stimulant is so different that many don't "feel it working", and therefore miss when it "quits working." Remember, with Vyvanse, look for the original cognitive, "mental" objectives, not the buzzy effects. When Vyvanse quits in the afternoon, the

ability to finish tasks is gone.

Summary: Using The Therapeutic Window

Start by setting DOE as a specific target; duration detection means precise, accurate dosing.

Make sure your medical team is in line with this objective.

Know your expected medication DOE before starting it.

Work to understand the specific ADHD objectives for each medication so that you can tell if they are corrected.

Watch for the afternoon drop to assess the Sides of the Window.

Use immediate release, generic meds in the same way as extended release, with clear ideas about the DOE for each type of expected DOE.

Remember that most second opinions, after months, even years, of not getting the meds right in the first place, are due to significant disrespect for these Therapeutic Window markers.

All psych medications can show changes through the day in the first weeks. As they say in Capistrano, California: One swallow doesn't make the summer.

Chapter 11
Breakfast Matters

Choose with care the rut you drive in,
- you'll be in it for the next 40 miles.

Road Sign Outside of Patagonia, Arizona

Nowhere does neuroscience come closer to everyday life than with the necessity of a protein breakfast. With or without ADHD, with or without ADHD medications, a nutritious protein breakfast will help with every aspect of any energy, cognitive or emotional complaints. And the science is firmly in place; it has been for years. Last time I checked, our brain and body are indeed connected; in fact, "you are what you eat"[46] and with the multiple high-glycemic seductions in the American diet, one can easily fall off the wagon. Most do with breakfast.

Put sugar in your gas tank, and you will gum up your engine. Put sugar in a car troubled with mixed-up timing and worn valves secondary to ADHD, and you will very likely trash your entire car. If you don't want to take medications in the first place, start with this breakfast chapter tomorrow morning, begin an exercise program[47] and get the right amount of sleep.

Breakfast, exercise, and, believe it or not, getting to sleep on time must become part of your maintenance process. All of these activities require a specific structure. If you want to correct your life with ADHD, the process requires far more than just medications changing your brain. You have to actually take care of your brain, mend your body and fire up your engine with the best food possible.

Picky Eaters: Set The Poor Breakfast Example

Take a minute to consider picky eaters and their relationship with breakfast. They don't eat breakfast, they cringe at vegetables and meat, and most often choose to eat only sweets and carbohydrates. You don't have to have a college degree in nutrition to know they have a problem, one that extends beyond weight gain.

See if you recognize this person: bright, sarcastic 17-year-old high school senior in advanced classes, failing in several because she is depressed and not getting her homework done. She does

46 McKeith, G, *You Are What You Eat*, 2006
47 Ratey, J *Spark: Exercise and the Brain*, 2008

not look sick or metabolically challenged on the surface, and regular medical reviews have pronounced her "healthy as a horse." She is from a caring, understanding family. She is cute, trim, looks like a cheerleader, is in the marching band, and isn't improving after many trials of medication for ADHD and depression. Bowel frequency: every other day, maybe.

Upon review she hides her breakfast aversion, is a picky eater across the rest of the day and is a serious carboholic. Urinary neurotransmitter review showed significantly diminished neurotransmitters, specifically dopamine and serotonin, even though she is on Vyvanse and Effexor XR, and showed a significant histamine elevation. She has had picky eating issues since childhood, and after further testing, clearly demonstrated allergies to wheat and milk proteins (gluten and casein). Removing the wheat and milk proved a challenge, but adding specific neurotransmitter precursors to her medical formula has completely turned her around after medications previously proved inadequate. She has improved, and is moving toward college. Some of the signs of surplus estrogen, with irregular periods, PMS and heavy cramping improved without specific hormonal intervention.

We found the right treatment because we explored her breakfast history and bowel frequency.

The Picky Eater Problem Complex

Picky eaters often have ADHD. And just as we have been discussing with ADHD, picky eaters often accumulate a menagerie of unpredictable troubles in a complex array of downstream, biologically-based medical issues. They stay away from food, but collect almost every odd symptom available.

Let's break down just a few of the basic clinical pictures.

As picky eaters, they manifest odd patterns of repetitive food intake, and miss large sections of a complete diet, most often breakfast. There must be a reason for this problem -- look for it.

Picky eaters often look weak, age faster, are always touchy emotionally and become more troubled with time.

They are often socially maladjusted with no energy for sustained action.

Bowel issues abound, from constipation to diarrhea. Transit time[48] often remains uncalibrated.

Hormonal issues, especially estrogen dominance with PMS, PMDD Premenstrual Dysphoric Disorder –- significant depression associated with menstrual cycles.

Polycystic ovarian syndrome (PCOS) frequently occurs in young adolescent women with carbohydrate picky eater preoccupations.[49] Think: Pop Tarts.

Look like bipolar: With PCOS, for example, women become regularly unmanageable, angry and feel like they are in a constant state of PMS due to the associated estrogen dominance.

Picky eaters are often developmentally delayed, and often suffer from malabsorption difficulties.

Picky eating started in childhood, but always looked like "attitude," not a problem.

Some desire weight loss, and striving for an attractive appearance can often hinder direct corrective action. Ever wonder why celebrities and athletes have so many interpersonal issues?

48 Transit time link: http://bit.ly/TTplan
49 PCOS: http://en.wikipedia.org/wiki/PCOS

Emotional issues abound: Depression, anxiety, cyclic moods and sleep issues.

Trichotillomania: Compulsively pulling the hair frequently associated.

Asperger's traits often appear with the suggestion that Asperger's will cover the underlying biologic diagnosis. Wrong. Biology must be measured.

Thyroid issues are often associated, even in adolescence for reasonsnoted in just a moment.

Adrenal fatigue is a serious potential outcome (measurable with serial cortisol samples) that can be corrected if treated correctly and early.

Neurotransmitters measured in the urine, plasma amino acids and neurotransmitter precursor imbalances are frequently so significant that ordinary psychiatric medications can't correct the symptoms.

And the most important, the most overlooked issue: immune dysregulation due to a variety of antigenic[50] insults, from food to heavy metals to phthalates in plastic bottles.

Picky eaters often have even more challenges, but let's take just a moment to see where we are going with just these picky complaints. Let's take the leap from the obvious challenges with picky eaters, to the subtler, but parallel and often carbon copy problems with just skipping breakfast.

The Bottom Line On Breakfast, Nutrition And Picky Eating

The easiest way to dive into this picky-eating-breakfast subject –- the simplest bottom line –- are three essential points

---

50 Antigenic defined: a foreign invader in the body causing an allergic reaction

that are almost completely ignored in the process of treating ADHD. Breakfast can become the canary in the coal mine for:

Immune dysfunction

Absolute neurotransmitter challenges

Underlying hormonal and nutritional deficiencies

Every one of these challenges often connects with hidden, measurable biological problems. Each can be considered through specific laboratory investigations and each is significantly correctable. The biology of eating problems is far more contributory to persistent failure than the psychology of those disorders. If biology is not corrected, the disorder will remain a struggle.

Picky Eaters And Immune Dysfunction

These immune dysregulations that we see so often in the office do have specific origins. Once identified, these can most often be corrected. The operational culprit for many of these challenges is allergens.[51] From mold, to wheat and milk, many of us inherited an inability to protect ourselves from these invaders. They enter our GI tract through eating, they enter our lungs through breathing, and they enter our skin through contact with the outside world. Allergens are the invaders of our body.

Imagine poison ivy in your bowel. You can't scratch it, and worse, it doesn't itch. But the blisters are there. You're regularly eating poison ivy; your bowel is breaking down in its ability to ward off the non-self invaders, and you develop a leaky gut because the integrity of your gut lining rusts out from all the chronic poison ivy abuse.

---

51 Allergen defined: Substance that can cause an allergic reaction

No, you aren't leaking fecal material into your peritoneal[52] cavity, but you are leaking peptides -- antigens and invaders into your blood stream where they set off alarms throughout your body, over many months, even years.

Science today is far beyond just considering the Feingold diet for ADHD. Now we can, and do, specifically measure allergic reactions to various food dyes and much more. The labs listed below tests for as many as 110 different antigens (including those Feingold food dyes), those invaders that make it past our body barriers. The science is firmly in place regarding gut challenges and immune dysfunction,[53] and to ignore it encourages more biologic challenges with ADHD treatment.

A Rusty Bowel

If your bowel is broken and not working properly you will, very likely, over time, gain three new obstinate problems:

Your liver is working overtime to take up the detox slack ordinarily handled by your healthy bowel. The result: your liver is constipated. A bulletproof liver results and psychiatric medications will prove unpredictable. Medications don't work as well for you.

Your immune system is defensively lit up, has its own internal memory, and starts creating challenges with your hormone communication system and your brain communication system with its neurotransmitters. Communications become rusty and broken on every major communication network in your body. You have hormone and immune challenges that test your

---

52 The space where your gut resides
53 Fasano, A, Shea-Donohure, T *Mechanisms of Disease: the role of intestinal barrier function in the pathogenesis of gastrointestinal autoimmune diseases* Nature/ Clinical Practice 2005

ability to cope. Remember: Your psychiatric medications don't work downstream from hormone or immune dysregulations. Hormone and immune system imbalances interfere with neurotransmitters.

Your neurotransmitter system depends (as do both of the other two systems) on proper nutrition for vitamins and minerals to keep all the cycles working for your energy and life activities. Most importantly for the brain, with a rusty gut you don't metabolize amino acids properly, and you can actually go into a neurotransmitter deficiency. With neurotransmitter deficiencies, guess what happens again: your psychiatric medications, which depend upon neurotransmitters to do their job, don't work.

The Absolute Neurotransmitter Challenges With No Breakfast

The jury of scientific review has come in long ago and rendered an irrevocable verdict: no protein at breakfast will significantly affect your entire day. Your brain works with neurotransmitters. Your brain doesn't work right without them. This point is common sense. You know it's true; the only problem is setting yourself up to take action. Your neurotransmitters numbers matter. Their absence means faulty neurotransmission -- depression, ADHD, sleep problems, etc.

Without breakfast over time, you will likely prove resistant to medications. You will be more likely to show increased ADHD symptoms as time passes, and your energy and interest in life will wane.

If you are a mother or father, your ADHD child or adolescent needs to advance more intelligently into adulthood with the proper nutritional, amino acid precursor equipment and healthy GI function. Without those essentials, the good grades they made under your care at home will dissipate in the vapors of a costly college conundrum. The time to register this concern with them is before the challenging age of fifteen, while they may still have some inclination to listen.

Without proper neurotransmitter balance, including both excitatory neurotransmitters such as dopamine and inhibitory neurotransmitters such as serotonin, the brain reacts to changing reality in an unbalanced way. Any brain activity, from thinking, to feeling and subsequent actions, can become impaired with faulty neurotransmitter balance.

Some Simple Protein Breakfast Solutions

These are basic ideas, and they have worked in my office. Nothing fancy here, just an attempt to help you with those early magic hours, even if you are in the military or on shift work and have to be at work at five in the morning. Get into the breakfast process. Get a calendar and keep score with yourself. Make a note on the days that you skipped it, and then reflect on your progress.

Take care of yourself; no one else will do it for you. It's surprising to me how often these options are ignored and how often the discussion about a protein breakfast is characterized by surprise and intense eye rolling.[54]

Protein comes in many easy packages. You can mix protein powder with your cereal or with oatmeal, and many who are working with their kids have enjoyed Spirutein's Cookies and Cream. Spirutein comes in many flavors, so go to GNC or the Vitamin Shoppe and find your favorite, from strawberry to

54 CorePsych Blog on Protein Breakfast: http://bit.ly/protbreak

pineapple.

I thought I invented an easy egg breakfast years ago, and several years after I began blogging about breakfast matters, a Zen student out in Idaho sent me a comment that her Zen Masters had been using this recipe for years, saying it was ancient and uniquely nutritious: stir two eggs in a bowl, add old-fashioned oats to form your preferred consistency, pour in your favorite extra virgin olive oil (keeps it from sticking too much), and put the bowl in the microwave for 1.5 minutes. Somehow I don't think the monks were using microwaves, but they knew that the combo filled you up, lasted well past noon and didn't take too much time out of meditation. I call this the Parker Power Protein Breakfast, with no intent to brand it. Looks terrible, tastes great, and you'll never know who will like it.

For the really touchy, consider a protein shake mixed with the berries of your choice. Blend it, throw in buffered Vitamin C and a tablespoon of virgin coconut oil, and you will then have the Parker Protein Polynesian. Sounds like a girlie drink, but I have a lot of guys that make this on their own, and I always tell them: your mom, your girlfriend or your wife will love you more for taking care of yourself. It should be a guy thing.

Carefully review the protein bars in your local pharmacy or grocery. My most recommended and most appreciated: Cliff Builder Plus and Think Thin. Both have 20 grams of protein, multiple great flavors and can be tossed down while running for the bus. These may not be your favorites, so just get something with 12–20 grams of protein with the fewest carbs possible.

If you are just too picky, try the low carb protein drinks. Those carry about 10 grams of protein and multiple flavors as well. If you have that bowel problem try flaxseed meal. Some grind their own flaxseed, and if you have an inclination to go that extra mile, it's the best way to go. The dose of flaxseed meal is two tablespoons in the morning, two if needed in the afternoon, more water and two chelated magnesium in the morning, two in the afternoon until you have a bowel movement.

A big glass of milk doesn't meet the protein requirement, peanut butter on crackers doesn't meet the protein requirement, and Fruit Loops or Frosted Flakes don't either. If we ever meet, don't bring it up if you do eat Pop Tarts; it will prevent an embarrassing lecture.

Eat a protein breakfast, exercise and get proper sleep. Your brain and body will run much better, last longer and will be happier.

If you're eating a good protein breakfast you might as well follow up with appropriate exercise as all of the studies point to improved recovery with fitness training.

Summary: Protein, Breakfast of Champions

These overlooked details will make your treatment with ADHD medications more successful. Follow the breakfast rules and you will have less medical bills, less frustration with medications and a clearer idea of how they work when you go in for a medication check.

Take the time to shop and experiment for the right breakfast food; get out of your rut.

With appetite decrease, the moods get worse in the afternoon, concentration is worse through the day, and the meds get blamed. Breakfast is quite often the correctable problem.

No breakfast + stimulant medications, often = no lunch.

No lunch and no breakfast means afternoon crashes will

intensify.

No breakfast creates significant problems with psychiatric medications entering too quickly into your system. I always give psych meds after breakfast and amino acid neurotransmitter precursors before breakfast for that very reason.

Remember all the psychiatric medications currently on the market only serve to modify neurotransmitters already in the body; they don't make or grow neurotransmitters.

With low neurotransmitters a variety of problems occur:

Meds wear out sooner and need more adjustments over time

Meds work more unpredictably

They require more cost in time and effort

Drops are bigger in the afternoon

Augmentation strategies with other meds don't work

Medications have a more narrow Therapeutic Window; the top dose is very close to the bottom dose

Discontinuation syndrome with antidepressants occurs more emphatically every time serotonin is diminished.

Tachyphylaxis: Adjustments are more necessary over time[55]

Moods often fluctuate no matter what psych meds you are using.

---

55 Tachyphylaxis defined: http://en.wikipedia.org/wiki/Tachyphylaxis

Chapter 12
Sleep For Brain Defrag

Sleep that knits up the raveled sleeve of care
The death of each day's life, sore labour's bath
Balm of hurt minds, great nature's second course,
Chief nourisher in life's feast.

Wm. Shakespeare, *Macbeth*

Without enough sleep, ADHD medication treatment cannot work. Lack of sleep will wash out any treatment over time, often a very short time, and changes in meds won't work because the brain is fragged. Sleep is the best brain defrag, better than drugs, more effective than a vacation.

If you have ADHD, and you have sleep problems and don't eat breakfast, your brain will not reset and you will remain seriously fragged.

Serious, advanced sleep fragmentation often results in psychotic thinking, hospitalization, bipolar symptoms and dangerous regressions. The more chronic the sleep problems, the fewer total hours slept, the more emotional regressions. ADHD can significantly contribute to sleep problems; that's why they must be treated as part of a comprehensive treatment strategy.

Even if you don't have a computer, just imagine a utility in the computer that will sort all of the cluttered desktop information stored there. If you do have a computer, take a moment to reflect on how long it takes for the defrag process. You can eat a sandwich while you wait. But your desktop speed will flash like lightning when you restart. It's the same with your brain, even your brain on ADHD.

What to ask yourself about sleep.

When do you sleep? Do you have trouble falling asleep? Staying asleep? Do you wake up too early?

Many say they don't have a problem until you confront them with specifics on Total Average Hours of sleep. These significant sleep challenges absolutely require more attention because chronic sleep deprivation at the very least will become associated with paranoid thinking and more fragmentation. Ask any police officer, firefighter, nurse, or physician with shifting night hours and taking excessive call. Paranoia and anger can result no matter how intelligent and sharp you are during the day.

Studies show that most of us should get 8.25 hours of sleep. I regularly tell my edgy adolescent patients, "I won't hold you to the .25!"

Do I insist on that number? The short answer is no, but I do shoot for it and work toward it with patients until we remove sleep insufficiency from the treatment equation.

Parker Learns About Sleep And Paranoia

During my adult psychiatric residency in Philadelphia, I worked at Albert Einstein Medical Center on Broad Street and had way too many irons in the fire. For side income I moonlighted at the Community Mental Health Center located at Friends Hospital once or twice a week. I was definitely stressed out and short on sleep, but in denial about it.

One night the Philly police brought a paddy wagon to Friends Hospital with an enormous, chained-and-handcuffed drunk, one with a famous last name. For this book we'll call him Picasso. He roared considerable epithets when we opened the paddy wagon door, so I slammed the door and told the cops to get him over to the hospital to get him in and sedated before he hit somebody, like me!

Over at the lock up, several cops and I wrestled him to the floor, and I gave him an IV injection meant to put him out for the night. He shuddered and breathed heavily, sighed and began to snore loudly, so I told the cops to unchain him, and we gathered our stuff and quickly left the seclusion room, and shut the door, none too soon. Suddenly he jumped up, ran to the unbreakable window in the door and shouted at me: "You no good ... hippie

... Communist ... pinko ... m..f!!

I felt safe outside the door and turned away thinking he would crash, and then he shouted, "Now I'm coming to get you!" He staggered back, ran at the door and hit it so hard it lifted the frame off the wall about an inch, then he hit the floor like a prize fighter on the canvas.

We sped in while he was down, and I shot him up with another full blast that put him completely out. We left him snoozing like a giant, drooling baby.

I went back over to the office sleeping quarters, climbed into my bed and absolutely could not sleep. I was already running on sleep deprivation, and I just could not get irrational, paranoid thoughts out of my head: He is still mad, could escape and would come and get me.

After about an hour of that I knew it was pointless to work at sleep anymore, so I got up to shoot the breeze with the night watchman, an interesting, unusual guy, who had been a heavyweight prize fighter, with great stories on many levels. That pugilistic conversation took me out of my mind rut, and I did get some sleep later that night. The point here is that sleep deprivation and near trauma can make even the psychiatrist paranoid.

Sleep Architecture

"Architecture" is a fancy phrase that simply indicates restful sleep. One simple test is to ask yourself, "Do I feel rested?" For many the answer is "no." Some reasons may be physical, such as adrenal imbalance, thyroid issues, physiologic stress and even malnutrition, or eating disorders.

Sleep Hygiene

I still laugh when I think of "sleep hygiene," but it's serious, and it often works. It's beyond crackers in the sheets, coffee or alcohol at night or even a late-night snack. Reduce the stimulation that will interfere with sleeping. Sleep Levels Need Evaluation: Level 1, falling asleep, Level 2, Staying asleep, Level 3, Waking up too early in the AM. Each level provides indicators for specific interventions based upon each specific sleepin pattern.

Estrogen And Hormone Testing

Estrogen dominance in young women is extraordinarily common. High estrogen levels almost always create problems in more than one of the levels of sleep. Untreated, they will ultimately create sleep problems in all levels.

The bottom line solution to these additional complexities: measure and correct estrogen challenges without simply resorting to birth control to regulate periods that seem uncontrollable. Birth control medications add estrogen! DHEA, an adrenal cortical hormone, can contribute to sleep problems; cortisol levels can corrupt sleep; progesterone deficiency can magnify a mild estrogen increase, and unidentified immune challenges with bowel problems can throw cold water on the entire treatment project.

Summary: Sleep Defrag Overview

Sleep medications, just as ADHD medication, should be used very specifically for the specific sleep correction objective.

Record your sleep problems at the outset in your recovery workbook. Know your sleep targets.

With your medical team, choose the best intervention, stick with it, and keep them informed of sleep challenges.

Use the half-life of medications for sleep, just as you do ADHD medications in the Therapeutic Window.

Desyrel most often works for Level 2 and 3, sometimes for Level 1.

Sonata works only for about 2 hours, will only work for Level 1 sleep and won't cover Level 2 or 3.

Restoril, a benzodiazepine, works for more than 8 hours, and is a useful benzo choice for the short term.

Tylenol PM and other over the counter meds frequently contain Benadryl, which often brings a hangover the next day. And, unknown to many, Benadryl blocks that 2D6 pathway that I discussed on the drug interaction chapter, causing stimulant accumulation.

Stimulant medications that affect sleep create that problem often because they are overdosed, and insomnia is a symptom of the Top of the Window.

Don't blame stimulant medications for pre-existing sleep problems. Often they can correct the night worries associated with ADHD.

Antidepressants and stimulants can both add to sleep problems. Many family doctors give Celexa, Lexapro and Effexor in the evening, and the antidepressant causes insomnia.

Estrogen dominance: Don't forget other important hormone measurements. Polycystic Ovarian Syndrome and other forms of estrogen dominance always have associated sleep issues, and psych medications don't fix hormone irregularities.

Fix the bowel and/or immune dysregulation, as those with either constipation, diarrhea or irregularity often have significant sleep problems.

Individuals who don't respond to stimulant medications, and then resist neurotransmitter precursors or amino acid supplementation, often are suffering with inflammatory cytokines (inflammatory communicators) and leaky gut problems.[56]

Sleep apnea is directly responsible for aggravating ADHD on several important levels.

---

56 More on precision and Turkey Shoots, http://bit.ly/tshoots

Chapter 13
Managing *With* Your Medical Team

The purpose of science is not to analyze or describe,
but to make useful models of the world. A model is useful
if it allows us to get use out of it.

Edward de Bono, Thinking/Creativity Consultant

Your medical team is just that, a team. If you don't, or can't, play as a team member, your care will suffer. So let's get some basics on the table before you take your next treatment steps. You can't do all of this by yourself, but you can do much more than you thought before we started.

Choosing Your ADHD Medical Team

What I am about to tell you is not meant to be offensive; it's just common sense. You won't get any use out of all this new science and all the suggestions in this book if you don't (or won't) work with your team and don't track your progress more specifically. Choose your team for affirmative correction of your ADHD progress, not to add an increased challenge or counterproductive dialogue.

To take this next step sometimes takes a revision of trust, an evolution with your medical team. You may have to rebuild or change your ADHD treatment team, so these are some thoughts in that regard.

Evaluate Your Current Medical Crew

Your current medical team may be conscientious in "things medical," but may not be interested in ADHD or psychiatric issues at all. If they don't have an abiding interest, if ADHD is a casual, rushed, or an afterthought, find another doctor. Switching will require some patience and searching.

ADHD isn't funny or casual. If your current medical team has a negative ADHD attitude, and, quite surprisingly, many do, don't try to talk them into taking care of your ADHD just because they render good medical care. Some who are great at medicine went into the field because they clearly did not like psych issues. Ask, and assess them on this point. They should be curious, interested in the complexity of these ADHD matters. A reticent attitude often proves frozen over time, certainly on the rapidly evolving subject of ADHD medication science. Attitude and information are connected.

In their defense, many family doctors are simply uncomfortable with psych meds because they don't use them regularly and simply don't have the protocol down for ADHD stimulants. With fears of legal consequences for addictive medications, it's a matter of choosing safety for their entire practice over taking those next learning steps. Stimulants are controlled substances, and family docs don't even like to write for small amounts of less tightly controlled psych medications, such as Xanax. Often they don't have office monitoring systems and worry about liability and abuse sometimes associated with scheduled substances.

If they don't want to learn the necessary basic information, don't want to grow their treatment process, and aren't curious about the pharmacology or comorbidity issues, that can impede your progress.

Over the years I have trained nearly twenty medical practitioners in my own practices, and I can tell you with absolute certainty that some just don't have the heart for working with ADHD. In retrospect I think some clearly reacted to its unexpected complexity.

I understand this apprehension from my own early medical experience. In the first year of medical school the Chief of Gross Anatomy, who also taught my mother and brother, said with deliberate gravity, "If you don't completely master Gross Anatomy, there will be a time in the future that the shingle on your door becomes an epitaph for a stillborn practice." Many know that only a little knowledge can become a dangerous trap down the line.

The Psychiatrist Problem

There are significant differences within the psychiatric community regarding treatment and understanding of ADHD. Many adult psychiatrists have the same attitude as the family docs. They don't "believe" in ADHD, don't come from a child psychiatry background with the exposure to childhood medication applications, and are significantly Paleolithic in their approach to stimulant medications. Many are still in absolute denial about the undeniable biology of ADHD.

Large sections of the country that, in a clear defensive move on my part, shall remain unnamed, are almost completely opposed to any change in medication practices, won't see pharmaceutical reps or ask questions that might show their marked deficits in basic ADHD diagnostic and treatment knowledge. Their reaction to new information: straight-out imperious.

These adult psychiatric practitioners appear to be awaiting word from academia on what to do next, since some clearly don't want to go down the ADHD path with insufficient information. This finding regarding adult psychiatrists is regularly reported by family practitioners and pediatricians when I visit their towns as they attempt to make treatment referrals.

So be prepared, you might see a counterproductive attitude with a diminished foundation of basic information, even within the psychiatric community. In such circumstances, the family docs and pediatricians don't know what to do, as they hear back unpleasant stories after thinking they had made a proper psychiatric referral. Health care management companies can also make it difficult for patients to pursue new avenues of treatment.

With consternation and real fears, even on the psychiatric side, it's easy to see why so many have many negative things to say about medications and treatment experiences with ADHD.

But as you can see from these pages, cheer up, it really isn't that difficult if you follow some basic *New ADHD Medication Rules*! So many of these matters can be solved using simple common sense mixed with the new science.

Go For Measurable Experience

Start with yourself, buy a workbook, outline your personal objectives, set a calendar, buy a pill buddy (plastic daily dispenser) if necessary for a reminder, and get serious about marking down your process.

First check your own attitude, then that of the team. Recovery takes serious attention, and a marked decrease in ambivalence.

Assess to see if your current medical team is up for the ADHD challenge. If not, consider moving on.

All of these comments involve setting up satisfactory feedback loops for informed ADHD action. Without give and take, the medications will remain imprecisely adjusted.

Plan to shop around for your team before you spend a nickel. You don't have to pay to see someone you don't like and don't agree with. I often get calls from individuals wondering if they could shop me up and ask a few pointed questions, and I always get back on my time. No problem.

If they don't want to talk beforehand, you don't need to see them. It's a bad omen for future customer service.

Ask about their experience and interest, and if they are comfortable with the ADHD problem you have to ask them about. If you have adult ADHD, ask the psychiatrist if he or she works with adult ADHD.

If you are wondering about a medication you may have read about, ask if they have experience with that medication. (Oddly, many are still not sure about Vyvanse at this writing, several years out from launch.)

Listen to friends who have seen the doctor in question. Our largest referral base has always, since I started practice, been friends and family.

Select a doctor who will listen, who has a game plan and who does not provide cookie-cutter medication protocols. You are an individual both emotionally and biologically, and it doesn't make sense to just take the meds on some routine scheme without explanation.

If you live in an academic town, recognize the fact that you may very well get better service from a nurse practitioner who goes to all of the meetings. Some in academia are surprisingly behind those experienced in the trenches, and too many live in the shadows of those hallowed halls worried they will offend their institutionally-thinking crowd.

Set Up Feedback From The Outset

Once in the office, simply address the process of how to communicate with your medical team: emergencies, urgencies, protocols and medications.

Remember, what you don't cover in the office, even with the most informed provider, you will have to handle yourself. Recovery is not a passive process where you go to be "taken care of." Rather, it's an active process of evolved mutual responsibility.

I recommend numerous handouts for every imaginable set

of tests and undertakings from **SPECT** imaging to laboratory testing, and written protocols for everything we do. If we don't have a protocol, we don't provide it.

Discuss breakfast and protein, and if they don't bring it up, just get into your workbook and write down objectives for yourself anyway.

Keep a record of the medications, the burn rates, any crashes and when they occurred in the day. As I indicated earlier, an afternoon problem is not necessarily a problem with the medication, but may be indicative of other problems not yet adequately addressed.

Regarding talking to your friends and extended family: keep your progress and your treatment to yourself. Everyone is an expert on ADHD medications and very, very few know anything about the biologic details. Bias against ADHD and the associated gossip prevail. You don't want more variables to interfere with your treatment, so keep it private, even with medical friends, many of whom remain in complete denial about ADHD challenges.

Take credit for your own progress. Your self-esteem always improves with self-mastery. Tell those who inquire that you have decided to change some things, but don't need to tell them exactly what you've done with medications. I've seen it flash back so many times on those casual with their personal ADHD information -- even a positive remark about their progress or their doctor can bring a truckload of speculation and doubt.

Summary: Team Work Overview

Your recovery is up to you; with this guide, you can make it happen.

Take your medications regularly. Go for the best and longest-acting medications, as compliance improves dramatically with fewer daily doses. You are worth it, and compromise on medication is not the best strategy, even though that may be necessary.

Switch your managed care policy if it remains a problem, and always complain to the medical director by letter. Remember, they aren't seeing patients, so they often have little idea of challenges at the front.

Manage your breakfast, your sleep, your metabolic rate, your exercise and your time to rest.

Don't fly off thinking you will fix everything in your life that you messed up all the years before by adjusting or increasing the medications. Stay within the guidelines so no problems arise with the Top of the Window.

Build your team with patience and the same understanding you want them to have for you. Respect goes both ways.

Give them this guide if they are interested.

Hopefully these pages will help you firm up the details of what can be a dramatically useful, life changing intervention for you or your loved ones.

Conclusion

Thanks for joining me through these *Rules* pages. I hope these different perspectives will lead to better paths on your personal journeys with ADHD medication challenges, and with your recovery from any associated biomedical difficulties.

If you have had some successes following reading *New ADHD Medication Rules*, I would appreciate your dropping a comment over at CorePsych Blog on this page http://www. corepsychblog.com/adhdbook. Your insights and observations will help others who struggle with the details.

If you aren't already involved with CorePsych Blog I invite you to join the conversation there. Stay tuned through CoreBrain.org for a variety of biomedical training opportunities regarding the many details not entirely covered here.

If you're interested in more information about neuroscience evidence do drop me a line at the office, review the page set up for specific learning modules, sign up for the CorePsych Insider newsletter and Administrative connections for CorePsych: http://www.corepsychblog.com/244

If you would like to learn more about me, my training and experience go to http://www.drcharlesparker.com

If you would like more information on neuroscience please see: http://www.corepsychblog.com/neuroscience.

And, finally, here are links to two laboratories that specialize in biomedical assessments: http://www.neurorelief.com and http://www.metametrix.com .

CPSIA information can be obtained
at www.ICGtesting.com
Printed in the USA
LVHW040329230523
747767LV00004B/61